Second Edition

MASTERING PEOPLE MANAGEMENT

Build a successful team – motivate, empower and lead people

Mark Thomas

THOROGOOD

Published by Thorogood
10-12 Rivington Street
London EC2A 3DU

Telephone: 020 7749 4748
Fax: 020 7729 6110
Email: info@thorogoodpublishing.co.uk
Web: www.thorogoodpublishing.co.uk

A CIP catalogue record for this book is
available from the British Library.

PB: ISBN 1 85418 328 1
    ISBN 978-185418328-6

Cover and book designed in the UK
by Driftdesign

Printed in India by Replika Press

The author

Mark Thomas BSc (Econ), DipPm, FIPD is a Senior Partner of Performance Dynamics Management Consultants, an international business consultancy specializing in change management, human resources and executive development. He also holds the post of Assistant Professor at the Tias Business School in Holland.

Prior to Performance Dynamics he worked with Price Waterhouse Management Consultants where he advised on the organization issues arising out of strategic change. His business experience encompasses mergers and acquisitions, privatizations and major restructuring initiatives. He currently manages a wide range of client assignments from business planning facilitation and organization reviews through to a wide range of executive development activities encompassing internal consultancy skills, team building and leadership development.

Previously he held a range of management roles in the information technology and food industries where his experience involved all aspects of organization development and human resource management.

Mark's work focuses on strategic change management and executive development. He facilitates business planning and top team events and runs a wide range of organization transformation programmes. He works throughout Europe, North America, Australia and the Far East and is a frequent conference speaker and writer on organization and human resource issues, having contributed to a number of books on organizational change. He was also previously Programme Director for Management Centre Europe's Strategic Human Resource Management Programme, and is currently Programme Director for a leading UK Mini MBA seminar. Mark's experience covers financial services, telecommunications, manufacturing, transport, information technology and local and central government. His clients include many major international and global corporations.

Mark was educated at the University of Wales and the London School of Economics and is a visiting faculty member of the University of Tilburg and their Tias Business School. He is also a Fellow of the UK Institute of Personnel and Development.

As well as writing many articles on business issues his books include:

- *Gurus on Leadership* (Thorogood, 2006)

- *High Performance Consulting Skills* (Thorogood, 2003)

- *Supercharge Your Management Role – Making the Transition to Internal Consultant* (Butterworth Heinemann, 1996)

- *Mergers and Acquisitions – Confronting the Organization and People Issues* (Thorogood, 1997)

- *Project Skills* (Butterworth Heinemann, 1998)

- *The Shorter MBA* (Thorsens, 1991)

He can be contacted at www.performancedynamics.org

Icons

Throughout the Masters in Management series of books you will see references and symbols in the margins. These are designed for ease of use and quick reference directing you quickly to key features of the text. The symbols used are:

 Key Question Guide to Best Practice

 Action Checklist Key Learning Point

 Activity Key Management Concept

We would encourage you to use this book as a workbook, writing notes and comments in the margin as they occur. In this way we hope that you will benefit from the practical guidance and advice which this book provides.

Contents

CHAPTER ELEVEN
Summary checklists 208

CHAPTER ONE

What is management?

What is management?

You are a manager! Welcome to the world of people management

The classic problems

About five months ago Jean Simons gained a promotion to a new managerial role. She had been a top class information systems designer and had earned a first class reputation as a technical specialist. It was on this basis that her boss decided to promote her into a management role. Jean herself was excited about the new role and the fact that it would provide, at long last, an opportunity to manage other people. Yet within two months of her appointment her team of six programmers and two designers were experiencing all kinds of problems and frustrations, and were soon complaining about Jean's management style. Jean herself attributed these difficulties not to herself, but to her clients' ever changing demands, but her team were only discussing one thing and that was Jean's inadequate people management skills. Relationships soon became strained and the performance of the unit started to deteriorate rapidly. Jean had made the transition from technical specialist and been welcomed to the world of people management.

James is a great salesman – top seller for the last six years – but the day we promoted him to sales manager proved a bit of a disaster. He has a team of six people working for him but he still manages to outsell them all, whilst in some cases their productivity has declined. His problem is he just does not manage his team. James has to learn to leverage his team and realize if he can get them working properly they will achieve far more than his individual efforts.

Carlos is a brilliant thinker and produces some terrific work but the turnover amongst his people is a real worry. Exit interviews with his people have identified a number of major problems with his management style. Whilst people generally respect his technical capability and experience they dislike his dominant 'I know best' attitude which results in him not listening to people and irritating the hell out of them. He will delegate work only to instantly be chasing people to see whether they have completed it. He does not appear to trust his people to really delegate.

Maria is a great accountant but she fails to deal with the issues amongst her team. She chooses to ignore the issues of poor performance and time-keeping with the result that human resources have to get involved at a later stage and we end up with much bigger problems. She just seems more comfortable with the technical side of her role and chooses to ignore the people issues.

Pierre's 360° performance appraisal feedback is dreadful. It appears to all that he is a real bully and has only one way to influence others, and that is to dominate them. People have accused him of talking over them, not listening, even shouting and banging his fist on the table!! I know he gets results but if this continues we are going to have to do something about him. He needs to recognize he has a problem and I am not sure he does at the moment.

As managers, the people skills we use on a daily basis are the major foundation of our business and career success – such skills effectively differentiate the superior leaders and managers. Yet most managers spend little time reviewing or developing their people management skills and practices. Today we work in complex organization and matrix structures where old levels of accountability are frequently blurred. We are tasked with having to generate new business, solve complex problems and look after an ever demanding workforce that has increased ambitions and expectations. Matrix structures are often difficult to work in and past levels of organizational accountability have often been surrendered to more ambiguous reporting lines. So the demands and pressures on managers are increasing all the time. Yet these day-to-day pressures frequently mean we have little time to stand back and analyze what it is we are doing. Often daily pressures mean we keep running without any reflection time. The danger of course is that we start developing dysfunctional practices and habits, and in today's competitive world this is a dangerous trap in which to fall. Any professional manager needs to be constantly reviewing and fine-tuning their people management skills. It is the major basis on which we can differentiate ourselves as business managers.

The effectiveness of the people who work for you is not solely determined by their individual competence, rather as much your ability to manage them – to motivate, develop and coach them! In turn your success as a manager is often determined by the way you manage your boss. In both relationships we need to ask whether we are given, and also provide, sufficient levels of autonomy, responsibility and guidance. Ultimately our leadership effectiveness is determined by our ability to develop strong working relationships and achieve high performance results through them. Ultimately business success is all about people and influence.

Against this background of rapid change many of our traditional approaches to management are under seige. Authority in today's organization is not automatically given to someone because of their position in the hierarchy. Knowledge and expertise have now gained currency at the expense of older styles of management that too often paid deference to rank and authority. People no longer expect or are prepared to carry out tasks simply because they are told to do so by a manager. People want to know the 'why' of an action, as well as the 'what'. No longer can any manager in any organization be confident that their past management performance will guarantee future success.

In order to succeed in today's fast changing organizations we need to demonstrate new approaches to influencing and gaining commitment from staff. We need to be open and willing to new ideas and approaches from anywhere. We might argue that this is not a new notion – managers have always had to be good listeners. But the need for higher levels of competence in influencing skills is now more critical than ever. Faced with increasing levels of global competition, organizations need to innovate and challenge conventional practices more than ever before. The global uncertainty facing organizations is greater than it has ever been and the need to share ideas and challenge within the corporate environment is a pre-requisite for survival. This requires managers to be comfortable in having their ideas constructively criticized; they need to resist taking offense or feeling that their authority or expertise has been called into question. For many managers this behaviour is not as easy as it might first sound.

Many organization cultures actively discourage people from challenging their managers. Many managers are deeply uncomfortable at the thought of having their ideas challenged or critiqued by junior staff. To do so in some organizations is to jeopardize your career path or continued development! The traditional approach is that managers are expected to manage and people are expected to follow. Yet the fact is that the vast majority of managers in organizations are still unable to sit down in front of their people and provide negative feedback in a construc tive manner! Until we have addressed this challenge we can perhaps forget fanciful ideas about becoming people centred learning organizations. However, this approach has to change, and is slowly changing. Mastering people skills is a big challenge for all individuals who aspire to become successful managers or leaders!

Projecting versus attracting strategies

When thinking about our own influencing and management style we have to recognize that we all have different strategies. We may not think of them as strategies but that is what they are. When we get out of bed in the morning we use different strategies. Some of us need just one alarm call and 30 minutes to get ready before we leave for work. Others need at least two or three alarm calls and a good hour and a half before they are ready. Conversely, some people need no alarm clock as they always wake up at the right time. In much the same way when we go into meetings at work we also tend to use different strategies. Some of us will be great listeners and reflect on what people are saying before we contribute. Other people will use a stronger approach making sure that their ideas are put on the table very early on in the meeting. They might then follow up by being very persistent in getting their ideas across by repeating and reinforcing their arguments. For some of us our strategies have become quite habitual and when we enter the world of management we may need to develop different strategies. Over time we all tend to develop a set of preferences and strategies about how we go about influencing others. One way of looking at these strategies and preferences is to highlight the difference between those of us who like to *Project* and those of us who like to *Attract*.

At one end of the spectrum some of us might be seen as aggressive and demanding, always pushing to get our own way regardless of the relationship costs involved. If we upset a few people in the process that does not matter so long as the job gets done. In meetings we will tend to push our own agenda and perhaps be very direct and even confrontational. If something is wrong we are not slow in pointing out the problem to colleagues. Others might describe it as being very blunt and lacking in diplomacy. Taken to an extreme this managerial behaviour or set of strategies can lead some to be described as domineering or autocratic. But in terms of influence these people do not have a problem with achieving influence over others. As strong *'Projectors'* everyone knows where they stand. The downside however is that *'Projectors'* may have difficulty in motivating people to follow them. They may be direct and forceful but when overdone they may in fact push people away. What they may need to do is develop some more attraction strategies to draw people towards their goals and aims. Projection is often a good strategy if you need to direct and secure compliance from others.

In contrast to the *'Projectors'* other managers might be described as more relaxed or laid back when it comes to dealing with people. They in effect operate strategies that might lead them to be termed *'Attractors'* – happy to go with the flow rather than force their own views. The *'Attractor's'* preference is to pull rather than push. People who employ lots of attraction strategies will typically be good listeners and inclined to let others have their own way at the expense of their own or some other specific business goal. This manager is frequently and rather unfairly characterized as a 'soft touch'. Individually they may feel frustrated that they should sometimes push harder and strive to get their own way more: but their approach is not to do so. In effect their frustration is created by their desire to try to develop some of the strategies of the *'Projectors'*. However, the benefit of good *'Attractors'* is that people generally feel comfortable with them and they can be good at collecting people as they will listen and seek to understand other perspectives. Attraction strategies are very effective at building commitment and followership.

PROJECTION AND ATTRACTION STRATEGIES

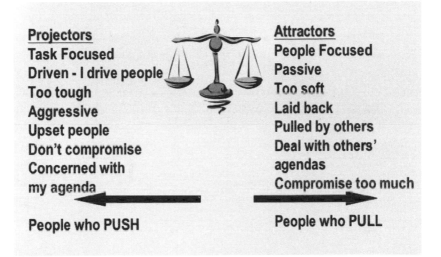

Projectors
Task Focused
Driven - I drive people
Too tough
Aggressive
Upset people
Don't compromise
Concerned with
my agenda

People who PUSH

Attractors
People Focused
Passive
Too soft
Laid back
Pulled by others
Deal with others'
agendas
Compromise too much

People who PULL

Of course neither of these two stylized sets of strategies are right or wrong. They just represent a different set of choices in how you might deal with other people. The key of course is to be able to achieve the right balance between the two. Knowing when to push and be direct but equally to know when to pull and listen is critical for any effective leader or people manager. In the real world very extreme 'Projectors' might be described as very aggressive and threatening. They often get a comeback as they invariably create lots of enemies who in turn seek some form of redress or revenge for the excesses of the 'Projector'. Conversely, the easy going 'Attractor' manager might lose out on opportunities because they might fail to 'project' strongly enough their own ideas or opinions. They might even be felt to lack the killer instinct needed to survive in the hostile and competitive corporate world. Either way you have to achieve the right balance.

CONTINUUM OF LEADERSHIP BEHAVIOUR

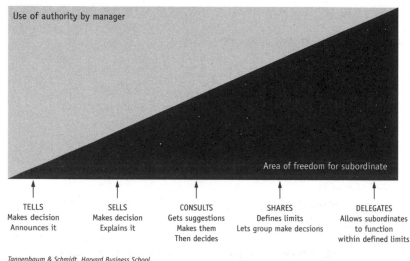

TELLS	SELLS	CONSULTS	SHARES	DELEGATES
Makes decision	Makes decision	Gets suggestions	Defines limits	Allows subordinates
Announces it	Explains it	Makes them	Lets group make decsions	to function
		Then decides		within defined limits

Tannenbaum & Schmidt, Harvard Business School

Early research and study into leadership style revealed the people and task dilemma that faces us as managers. In the late 1950s and 1960s two highly influential models were developed which characterized fundamental management styles. In 1958, R Tannenbaum and W H Schmidt wrote an article in the *Harvard Business Review* entitled 'How to choose a leadership pattern'. This definitive text characterized the classic management styles and was very significant in shaping thinking about leadership and people management. In the late 1960s Robert Blake and Jane Mouton, two American psychologists, developed their famous managerial grid which characterized the task and people continuum facing managers. In the Blake and Mouton model, managers were essentially characterized by their focus on the task and people dimensions. The grid outlined a number of stylized management styles.

Their model suggested that the ideal was a 9.9 type manager who combined a high task and productivity focus with high levels of people support and enthusiasm. In effect, someone who combined good projection and attraction strategies to both provide direction and also commitment and motivation. What we need to do as managers and leaders is develop a flexible and responsive people management style to enable us to deal with different types of people in different situations.

BLAKE/MOUTON MANAGERIAL GRID

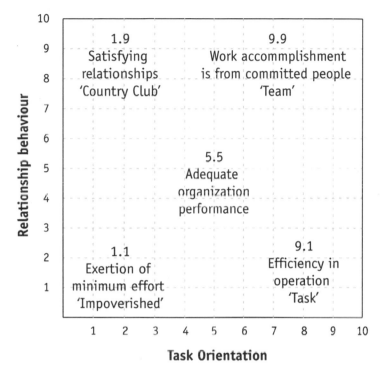

So what is management really all about?

The need for management in the business world normally arises when a group of people come together to tackle a task that is too large or complex for any one individual to cope with. When we are faced with such situations we soon discover that we may need to define tasks and allocate roles in order to develop an effective solution. The process of breaking tasks or problems down into key elements traditionally involved the classic management practices of Planning, Organizing, Staffing, Directing, Co-ordinating, Reporting and Budgeting – or the acronism POSDCoRB as it became known. These activities make up the key elements of most traditional and classic management roles.

The classic functions of management

The planning function

Planning involves establishing the main objectives or outcomes of the work. It entails detailing the tasks that need to be achieved and the methods for accomplishing them. Planning provides a strong focus and framework for any project or task. It comprises the following elements:

FORECASTING

Estimating future needs and requirements. For example, market growth, market share, customer demand, profit and revenue streams, return on investment etc.

ESTABLISHING OBJECTIVES

Establishing the results that have to be achieved. For example, increasing production, sales, profitability, reducing costs by x% or service response times by y%.

SCHEDULING

Establishing the priorities and sequence of actions needed to achieve the stated objectives. What is the order in which tasks and initiatives need to happen?

BUDGETING

Allocating the necessary resources to deliver the objectives and outcomes – people, equipment and finance. For example, a financial budget of $1.5 million and a project team of 22 people supported by eight contract workers.

ESTABLISHING PROCEDURES

Developing and applying standardized methods and processes for executing the work. For example, what project management or process control systems will be used to drive the project?

The organizing function

This function involves establishing formal structures of authority so that tasks and activities can be defined and co-ordinated amongst the people involved. Organizing also includes the selection and training of staff to deliver the objectives.

SELECTING THE TEAM

Identifying the right people with the right skills for the tasks and roles to be performed.

DELEGATING

Allocating the appropriate levels of responsibility and accountability to people.

ESTABLISHING THE WORKING CLIMATE

Creating the right working atmosphere for the development of strong working relationships and high performance team working.

The directing function

These activities involve:

DECISION MAKING

Making effective decisions in a timely and appropriate manner.

COMMUNICATING

Creating a shared understanding of the key goals and objectives through the use of appropriate communications channels.

MOTIVATING AND ALIGNING PEOPLE

Energizing people on a collective basis and leading them to deliver high levels of performance even when faced with setbacks and obstacles.

DEVELOPING PEOPLE

Advising team members on how they can fully develop their skills and capabilities to increase their value and realize their full potential.

The controlling function

This function involves monitoring any work in progress so as to ensure results are ultimately delivered. It entails inspecting projects and work plans and driving any financial planning, accounting or controlling procedures. The function also involves advising and reporting to senior managers on progress.

ESTABLISHING PERFORMANCE STANDARDS

Establishing the criteria by which work processes, tasks and results will be assessed and measured.

MEASURING PERFORMANCE

Recording and reporting on progress to see if the work is meeting the required time, cost and quality requirements.

EVALUATING PERFORMANCE

Evaluating and appraising the work and results achieved.

CORRECTING PERFORMANCE

Taking timely and corrective action to improve working methods and performance results.

The POSCoRB model of management has had a huge influence on management thinking and has resulted in many of today's standard management practices. The manager as a controller and director of people and resources has been applied in most organizations for the last few decades.

But things are changing

Whilst these basic models have had a big impact in shaping the way we think about management, there has in the last decade been a major shift away from some of the central foundations of traditional management thinking. Intense global competition and new technologies are providing complex new challenges to those who seek to build and sustain leadership positions. The entrance of China, India and Russia into the global economy is resulting in seismic shifts in the business world. Organizations are having to address fresh challenges with new perspectives and principles of organization thinking:

- **Fast responses**: how do we reduce the time delay between identifying and satisfying customer needs?

- **Continuous innovation**: what does it take to ensure that we continue to bring new ideas, products and services to market faster and more cost effectively than our competitors?

- **Customer satisfaction**: what does it take to get close to our customers and to deliver satisfaction at the right cost?

These challenges are forcing organizations to radically rethink the role of management. Faced with the need to do more and more with less and less resources means the traditional perspective of management as a controlling and directing function has been under attack. Many of the world's leading organizations now want their people to be self-directed. Words such as empowerment require people to be trusted to get on with their jobs without reference to continuous supervision or management. These new perspectives have major implications for traditional managerial roles.

The basis of this new order is that it is no longer viable for organizations to have lots of management roles and layers checking and controlling what other people do. If your organization is facing immense challenge from high quality and low cost global competitors and you have a business model that is based on lots of managers performing limited 'value added' roles then you are going to lose the war for global success. Your costs will be too high, you'll be slow to market and you'll demotivate talented people. Ultimately your organization will not survive!

Managing in the knowledge era

The fundamental question in this process of transition is a simple one: if we have got the right people with the right skills and motivation, then why do we need people wandering around and checking up on them? Accordingly many leaders have now redefined their expectations of day-to-day management. Taking personal responsibility for your day-to-day actions is the current mantra. This approach acknowledges the major shifts that have occurred in the world of work. Traditional notions of what constitutes value in the organization, such as capital and plant equipment, are rapidly, if not already, being replaced by the notion of **intellectual capital** that places a premium on brands, skills, imagination and people capabilities as the sources of competitive advantage. This approach demands a very different concept to managing others. Instead of checking and controlling, the manager is expected to act as an enabler and facilitator of talent – in effect they assume the role of a coach. This need to empower people to take responsibility for their actions will only accelerate in the face of relentless global markets and competition.

**NEW ORGANIZATION STRUCTURES DEMAND NEW
PEOPLE MANAGEMENT APPROACHES**

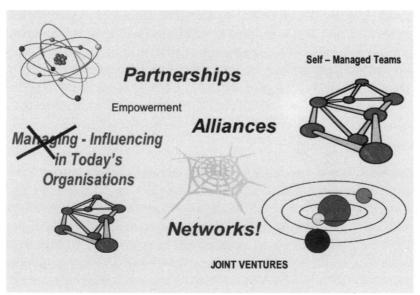

This new model for management requires people who have:

- A high level of interpersonal skills and an ability to communicate, motivate and mobilize others towards common and shared goals.

- The ability to create a positive working atmosphere in which people feel free to communicate their ambitions and ideas but who also feel comfortable raising concerns and challenging others, even their boss.

- The ability to involve people in decision making processes and secure their commitment to any stated aims and objectives.

The knowledge era also requires managers who are comfortable working on strategic activities and with conceptual thinking. They need to deal with abstract concepts more than ever and must be able to view the organization as a total system, rather than through narrow functional perspectives such as sales, finance, information technology or production. The ability to use conceptual thinking skills is critical as it raises peoples horizons above day-to-day operational thinking. You have to be able to view the wider corporate, market and business environment. Many managers have lost out in terms of career development and advancement if they were judged to be lacking in a strategic perspective. But today such skills apply to any executive in any organization, regardless of their position. The fact is that in this knowledge era the emphasis for managers is on thinking, not doing! For many of us this is the great challenge as we often fall into the trap of confusing being busy with being effective. Too often in today's business world we don't have time to think, it is all about getting on and getting the job done. But the fact is that thinking skills carry a premium in today's business world.

Adapting the process of managing to the knowledge era

To understand management in this new knowledge era is to view it as a dynamic process that consists of four critical stages: Setting the direction, Empowering, Enabling, and Reviewing.

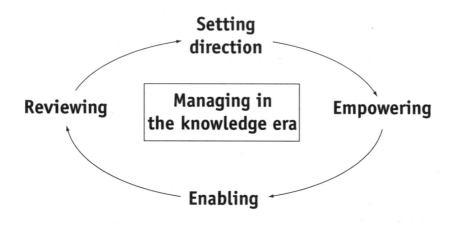

These four stages might be described as follows.

Setting the direction

This involves setting out the big picture and future business direction. Providing focus and a compelling vision for people is one of the critical differentiators of effective leaders. It requires us to engage people so as to secure their commitment to the stated goals and objectives. Drawn from the classic POSCoRB model this process retains the essential elements of setting out and then agreeing the results that need to be achieved.

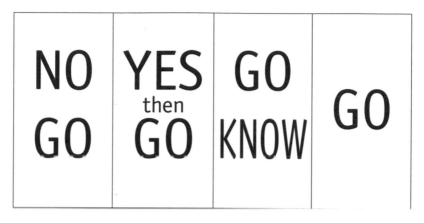

Empowering others

Empowerment became one of the great buzz words of 1990s corporate life. But few people really understood what it meant and as a result it became a much abused word. Essentially empowerment is not about giving people limitless freedom to do whatever they want, but rather a process for providing people with clear levels of accountability and responsibility. Mark Brown an author and consultant has developed a very elegant model to clarify this concept. It provides a way in which we can audit our approach to delegating responsibilities to staff. Using his model, managers simply need to be clear with their people on the following areas:

- **No Go.** These are areas or tasks that staff have no responsibility or involvement with – they are the strict domain of the manager.

- **Know Go.** These are areas or issues where, provided the manager involved has been consulted and given permission to the individual to proceed, they can then act – but they must get authorization beforehand.

- **Go Know.** This involves tasks or issues whereby someone can act but they have to keep their manager advised of what they have done. Significantly though, the notification of what was done does not need to be reported before or immediately after the event. It can be done through a later meeting, email or formal report.

- **Go.** This is the field in which people can act without any reference to their manager – they are empowered to act without reference to their manager or boss.

Enabling others

A leader or manager who 'enables' others ensures that people have the necessary level of resources and capabilities to deliver their agreed objectives. To 'enable' as leader or manager we will be communicating fully with our people and attempting to free them from unnecessary organizational obstacles or interference in order to allow them to deliver results.

Reviewing performance

The final stage of our management process involves reviewing performance and taking corrective action for future performance improvement. This is not about simply checking up on people but rather it involves a detailed discussion with the team and individuals to see if the best possible results have been achieved. It will also identify any learning from the experience and possible new opportunities to improve future performance. To make all of this happen we need to become accomplished people managers.

Under this empowerment model we are, as effective leaders, required to generate the optimum organizational conditions to enable people to flourish and grow as unique individuals. The focus is on cultivating a clear and guiding sense of individual worth, responsibility and commitment to the overall organizational vision. This is in contrast to an organization that has a dependency culture whereby people are unable to function without a manager constantly directing proceedings and checking up on them. Of course broad direction still exists in our model but the focus is very much allowing the individual to become self directed. Again the manager's role becomes that of a coach and facilitator.

Two classic approaches to managing and leading in today's organization

To get us to think further about these themes there are two classic leadership models that can assist us in a very practical way. Both these models were originally developed some 30 years ago. This may provoke the response *"Then how can they be useful to us today"* but these models remain as powerful and useful today as when they were first introduced. Both help us as leaders and managers to understand the dynamics involved in 'letting people go' to develop their real capabilities – the challenge in leading today's organizations.

ACTION-CENTRED LEADERSHIP

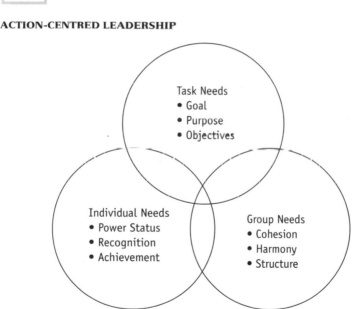

John Adair's Action Centred Leadership Model and Paul Hersey's situational approach are famous for helping managers think about their individual style and have been applied in thousands of organizations around the globe. The high emphasis that both these models place on delegating and trusting people to achieve superior performance is clearly aligned to the notions of empowerment and enabling people.

John Adair is a highly distinguished academic, consultant and author. He studied history at Cambridge University and holds higher degrees from the universities of Oxford and London. After Cambridge he became senior lecturer in Military History and Leadership Trainer Adviser at the Royal Military Academy, Sandhurst. In addition to consulting with major companies he works with numerous government bodies covering every field from education to health.

In a distinguished career studying leadership, John Adair has described leadership as akin to balancing three critical dimensions at the same time. These dimensions represent the core of management and relate to the emphasis any leader places on:

- Achieving the task or goals. *Task*

- Developing individuals and their capabilities. *Individual*

- Building a team out of a group of individuals. *Team*

The essence of Adair's approach is that these dimensions must be managed if leaders are to be effective. Success, he argues, cannot be achieved in isolation. Well developed individuals need to work together as part of a successful and functioning team. Similarly teams are not effective if they don't complete tasks on time and achieve their objectives and goals. So, if as a leader we neglect one of these three dimensions we need to recognize that it will impact on the other two. A team that is not focused may soon develop poor working relationships and, in time, this will invariably impact on their ability to complete key tasks and deliver results.

Adair is also a strong advocate that leadership skills can be taught. He places great emphasis on the notion of **leadership effectiveness** which he describes as **what we do as opposed to who we are.** This is a very powerful distinction to make as many people believe that you can't be a leader unless you have a certain kind of charismatic personality. Indeed, many people develop blockages in their mind because of this kind of thinking. Some people will say to themselves, "I'm not a good people manager!" or "I don't do the touchy feely stuff". **Adair reminds** us that leadership is about what we do as opposed to who we are. He argues that if we carry out the activities that accompany his model then people will soon begin to increase their leadership effectiveness. His model allows us to analyze whether or not we actually carry out the activities his model details.

Action-centred leadership – a checklist

- Define the fundamental mission and objectives of the team: Why do we exist? What are our key aims and goals. Provide a clear sense of purpose and direction – the vision.
- Communicate the vision and team goals with real enthusiasm.
- Set out and agree clear roles for individuals. Communicate those roles.
- Focus individuals on their key tasks and objectives.
- Set individual targets after discussion and consultation; discuss individual progress with each team member.
- Work in teams of four to 15 people and ensure people understand the three dimensions of Task, Team and Individual.
- Ensure the continuing commitment of individuals to the team.
- Review and replan when necessary and check on progress with the team.
- Delegate decisions where possible to encourage responsibility and accountability.
- Consult with people on important issues or decisions.
- Communicate the importance of everyone's role.
- Brief the team regularly on important developments – successes, problems, people issues etc.
- Constantly train and develop people.
- Demonstrate care for the well-being of team members; constantly seek to improve the working environment.

- Deal with any grievances promptly.
- Monitor progress; learn from successes and mistakes; practise Managing By Wandering Around (MBWA), observe, listen and praise people.
- Have fun!

CHECKLIST: LEADERSHIP THE JOHN ADAIR MODEL

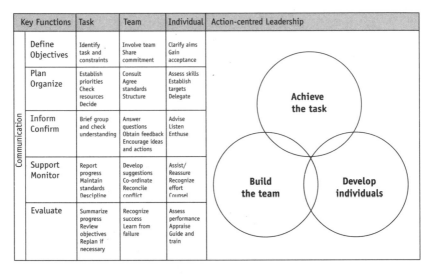

Key Functions		Task	Team	Individual	Action-centred Leadership
Communication	Define Objectives	Identify task and constraints	Involve team Share commitment	Clarify aims Gain acceptance	
	Plan Organize	Establish priorities Check resources Decide	Consult Agree standards Structure	Assess skills Establish targets Delegate	
	Inform Confirm	Brief group and check understanding	Answer questions Obtain feedback Encourage ideas and actions	Advise Listen Enthuse	
	Support Monitor	Report progress Maintain standards Descipline	Develop suggestions Co-ordinate Reconcile conflict	Assist/ Reassure Recognize effort Counsel	
	Evaluate	Summarize progress Review objectives Replan if necessary	Recognize success Learn from failure	Assess performance Appraise Guide and train	

Task, team and individual model

1 Achieve the task	2 Build the team	3 Develop individuals
• Define goals and tasks	• Share responsibility	• Delegate tasks and responsibility
• Check the resources and capabilities available	• Consult with people	• Coach people
• Set clear standards of performance	• Encourage people	• Promote trust and integrity

1 Achieve the task	2 Build the team	3 Develop individuals
• Brief people	• Respond to questions	• Recognize excellence and commitment
• Check team understanding	• Solicit and provide feedback	• Appraise and reward performance
• Manage time constraints	• Co-ordinate efforts	• Train people to fulfil their potential
• Recognize priorities	• Manage conflicts	• Listen to people all the time
• Be decisive	• Recognize successes	• Coach and counsel people
• Monitor and report on progress	• Encourage creativity and innovation	
• Review objectives	• Allow people to take risk	
	• Use humour	
	• Learn from successes and failures	
	• Have fun and celebrate	

The situational approach

Dr. Paul Hersey is a behavioural scientist whose ideas have been used to train managers around the globe for more than 30 years. Founder and CEO of the Centre for Leadership Studies, he has helped train more than four million managers from over 1,000 organizations worldwide. Hersey originally worked with Ken Blanchard (of *The One Minute Manager* book fame) to produce the highly influential situational approach matrix. Their main contribution to the study and understanding of leadership and management was to break the myth that there is one ideal leadership style for all situations. Rather, managers and leaders need to adapt their leadership style to different situations. A common sense notion but what the model then proceeds to do is provide a very practical approach to achieving the right balance between the art of controlling and delegating.

Hersey asserts that two major factors influence how we manage as leaders:

- *The emphasis we place on any task being completed.* The more we stress the task dimension the more directive our leadership behaviour will be. A strong task focus will mean we specify what we want done, how we want it done and the time in which it needs to be done. Highly task focused managers leave the person having to do the work with little, if any, discretion in how they complete a task or job. The task focused leader sets the pace and direction.

- *The emphasis we put on the relationship with people and the amount of support we give them.* The more we stress this dimension then the more supportive our leadership and management behaviour will be. In a highly supportive mode we encourage and praise good work and develop close and supportive working relationships with colleagues and team members.

Leadership: the most valuable attributes of a leader

TELLING STYLE • HIGH TASK – LOW RELATIONSHIP

- Those of us who use this style effectively control the work of our staff closely. We act quickly to correct and redirect any performance shortfalls. We make sure staff are clear about what they have to do and stress the importance of their targets and deadlines – emphasizing the use of standard operating procedures. Typical comments might include:

  Let me be clear as to what it is I want you to do.

  I will explain precisely how this work must be completed.

  You then need to ensure that you have contacted x. Do you understand fully what it is I am asking you to do?

SELLING STYLE • HIGH TASK – HIGH RELATIONSHIP

- If we use this style we tend to show a concern both for the task as well as people relationships. Utilizing this style we will spend time in positive and supportive dialogues but also ensure that people are clear about their responsibilities and the required standards of performance. This style will also seek to incorporate and might utilize staff suggestions but ultimately the manager retains full control over how a task is completed. Typical comments might include:

  This is a great opportunity for you to learn something new so let me explain what you need to do...

  Thanks for coming in today I am pleased to be able to get you involved in this important project as I think you can learn a lot from it. So let me outline what you need to do.

PARTICIPATING STYLE • LOW TASK – HIGH RELATIONSHIP

- The manager who uses this style lets staff organize and manage their own work plans following a dialogue. Participative managers allow people to set their own goals rather than adopting a directive task focused approach. Such a style also encourages and supports positive staff ideas and contributions.

- This manager will be available for discussion and advice, but will not push their involvement. They try to minimize the need for direction and will work hard to make staff feel valued and involved in the process. Staff are encouraged to determine their own roles and priorities, with guidance being available if requested. Typical comments might include:

So I have outlined the problem, what are your ideas as to how we might approach the customer with the issue?

So what do you think about the challenge?

I would be very interested to hear your comments as to the way ahead?

DELEGATING STYLE • LOW TASK – LOW RELATIONSHIP

- When we delegate we effectively let staff address any problems and formulate solutions for themselves. When we delegate we do not intervene unless we are asked for help or unless our assessment or monitoring processes lead us to think there may be a problem – in which case we can switch to a participating style of management. Typical delegating statements might include:

So I am going to hand over the problem to you!

I guess you can get on with that project without help from me – but I'm available if you need to discuss any issues.

Here's a new assignment for you to carry out. Let me know if you want to discuss anything, otherwise I'll leave it to you.

By utilizing the model we come to recognize that there is no generally accepted 'best' style. Rather the model urges us to think about matching the 'best' style to any given situation. The situational approach argues that in order to be truly effective managers, we need to adapt our style according to the maturity of the people who have to carry out the actual task. Hersey defines maturity into two distinct elements:

- **Motivation**. Is the individual motivated and willing to undertake and complete the work or task they are being asked to undertake?

- **Competence**. Is the individual competent to do the work? In other words, do they have the necessary level of knowledge, skills and experience to complete the task?

Based on the answers to these questions an effective manager then chooses the most appropriate style to the given individual and situation. The model then points us to using four classic leadership styles:

The telling style

- Where people have low levels of competence and low levels of motivation this suggests that close management supervision is required. Otherwise we might discover that the work may not be completed to the required standard or time limitation. In some cases an individual may lack confidence in addition to not possessing the skills to complete a task. In such cases a manager will need to spell out in detail what needs to be done and show how it needs to done in order to give the individual confidence and the skills to get the work done. If you think about some new staff it is essential that close attention is paid to clarifying their roles, responsibilities and any limits of discretion when it comes to completing any new tasks. Attempts to use a participating or selling style of management may prove less effective. Whilst good relationships may be established, people still need to have a clear understanding of their job and what is expected of them. So a telling style is a perfectly legitimate approach to adopt with people who don't have the right experience, confidence or motivation to complete a task. You need to be directive and spell out in detail what is required.

The selling style

- If we are continually directive and constantly use a telling style towards people they will soon become resentful and demoralized, particularly if they are smart and motivated. A relentless telling style might provoke a "My boss thinks I am an idiot!" type response. As a result some people might eventually leave the organization. In other cases they might be unwilling to take on further responsibility – *why should we make any decisions, the boss always tells us what to do*! Longer term implications of this approach might also cause the boss to work longer hours as they struggle to keep up with ordering people what to do all the time. Equally, on return from holiday the boss might find nothing has happened as people have developed too high a dependency on them for direction and decisions.

So, as someone matures in a role and shows enthusiasm, as effective managers we will want to further encourage them to do more by providing a supportive and friendly approach. Conversely, if someone lacks the right competence or skills to complete a task we will still need to be directive if we are to get the outcome we need. So we still have to be task focused but seek to combine it with a high level of relationship support to encourage and respond to someone's enthusiasm. For a manager to jump to the next level and use a participating style will fail because the individual still fundamentally lacks the skills or experience to address the problem under their initiative.

The participating style

- As people become increasingly competent and motivated, we no longer need to emphasize the importance of the task element in directing work – competent people already know what they need to do and how to do it – so we can concentrate on establishing strong supportive working relationships. This participating style enables us to keep in touch with the individual and their work. If necessary we can easily move back to a selling style to correct any performance problems that relate to competence or experience. A prime benefit for the manager in moving into a participating style is that it is far less time consuming as you are no longer having to tell people what to do all the time as their competence level is starting to be optimized. When we are in the participating zone we are really getting into the coaching and facilitating role of leadership. Essentially we are growing people into a high performance role.

The delegating style

- A high level of staff maturity is reached when an individual is both highly skilled and highly motivated: a manager can, in effect, delegate and withdraw from any form of supervision leaving the individual to get on with it unless advice is sought. This approach also has an added motivational impact as high performance people will respond further to the additional responsibility. This of course is the ideal zone in which we all want to be able to operate as it allows us to get on with our real role as a leader which is to think about the longer term future – safe in the knowledge that our people are highly capable.

The situational approach also helps us understand that if there are performance problems, we can simply move back to a different style – from participating to selling. Equally, if an individual's performance is good, a manager can advance – from a telling to participating style. Consistency of approach is important, however, as too many style changes can create confusion and uncertainty amongst staff. The worst management habit is to continually jump from one end of the spectrum to the other. Classically this involves jumping from participating to telling and back again. Not surprisingly, such managers complain frequently about the unwillingness of their staff to assume responsibility, whilst staff complain about being confused and de-motivated. If you have a task delegated to you and the moment there is a problem your manager starts telling you what to do, it is confusing to be on the end of such a shift in approach. Of course to have delegated in the first place your manager must have assumed that you were both skilled and motivated. But if they then start 'telling' you what to do they are of course working on the basis that you are unskilled and not motivated or confident. The situational approach helps us appreciate the motivational impact of this type of sudden shift in style.

Management style is a complex and difficult area. Few of us get it right all the time. The situational approach provides a powerful methodology for managers to assess both their people and tasks in order to choose appropriate and successful leadership styles.

THE SITUATIONAL APPROACH APPLICATION • FOUR STYLES SUMMARY

- Telling — Highly directive and suitable for individuals who are either:

  1. New to their work and need to be supervised.

  2. Will not perform the task unless directed to do so – namely unwilling people.

- Selling — Very directive and supportive. Ideal for individuals who do not yet have the necessary level of capability (skills, knowledge and experience) but who are motivated, and as their manager you want to further encourage their commitment and confidence.

- Participating — For individuals who have the right skills and experience but who may need some additional relationship support to build their confidence and motivation, e.g. the newly promoted manager – you know they can do it but you may need to draw solutions out of them.

  Counselling issues – to find out any problems – why is someone who is experienced and able not willing to do something? For example, they are bored, feel let down by the company in some way etc. You have to discuss the problem to get to the solution – you need to participate.

- Delegating — For highly skilled, experienced and motivated individuals who know what they are doing! They are there – A team players who can be trusted to get on with the job without management direction!

- Directive   Giving individuals clear task instructions or directions about how, when and where they complete any specific tasks.

- Supportive   Listening and encouraging people to perform well. Securing their involvement and gaining their commitment. Being available to coach, counsel and guide.

Will managers become extinct?

Many people are naturally disturbed by any discussion that raises the basic worth and value of their job or role. But some organizational commentators have indeed been arguing that many managerial jobs as we currently know them face extinction. Of course the truth is probably somewhere in between. There will probably always be a need for managers who are involved in activities that involve setting direction and shaping the future of organizations. At the same time in large enterprises there will always be a need for some people to provide some form of direction and co-ordination at an operational level.

Yet it also seems clear that there will be a reduced need for the sorts of managers that we have had in our past organizations. Accelerating advancements in communications and information technology are enabling organizations to radically rethink their internal processes and structures. Technology is allowing work to be executed anywhere – location is becoming less of an issue. IT and back office functions are being outsourced to all corners of the globe. New information technology systems also allow people to work without the need for close managerial supervision.

Against this background any future manager in any organization might reflect on the following questions:

Are you placing too much emphasis on securing a management role? – after all it is only a title.

What do you do besides telling people what to do?

How do you add real value to the organization?

If you lost your management role tomorrow what would you do? What could you do?

Would you be better to hold onto your technical skill set rather than migrate to the world of management?

In the future, technical, market, customer or information technology skills may well serve us better than any simple set of managerial skills. Any role including management is simply a function of how an organization or business chooses to operate. Most customers have no interest in how you organize your business, they only want the right product or service at the right price.

So what is the new management skill set?

Managers in the future will be judged more on their ability to align and motivate people. The need to deliver results will remain paramount but managers will increasingly need to deliver on both measures – business results and people management. Managers who achieve results at the expense of people will be increasingly marginalized.

Managers wanting to use the Adair and Hersey models will need to get into the Individual, Team and Delegating spheres of activity. Encouraging people to become self sufficient and to work under their own powers of motivation will be the guiding force. Listening and putting people at the centre of competitive activity will become critical management endeavours. This will require managers who are comfortable in operating without the trappings of existing organization life. People skills are in!

The need to develop new and radical approaches to managing is not borne out of a sense of well-being towards people. It is a case of economic survival! The fact is, if I can operate with two layers of management and you need five I will kill you on costs. Plus, I will get my new products and services into the market place faster. Whereas you have to get them through all that bureaucracy, game playing and politics. So good luck and watch out that the competition don't innovate you out of existence.

Characteristics of the knowledge era and the worst of the old world managers

The knowledge era managers are:

- Interested in your role
- Supportive and excellent listeners
- Aware of your role and capability
- Not interfering
- Decisive
- Enthusiastic
- Flexible and willing to change
- Available to their people
- Able to set clear objectives
- Results focused
- Open-minded
- Willing to develop and grow people
- Able to develop high levels of trust
- Good at letting go

- Strong communicators
- Sincere – they never tell lies
- Approachable
- Keen to hear your views and ideas
- Balanced in their moods and disposition
- Consistent and positive in their actions
- Self-motivated – this 'rubs off' on people
- Interested in your opinions and views

Old world managers are:
- Ineffective communicators
- Bad listeners
- Indecisive
- Always changing their minds
- Suspicious of their staff
- Not interested in developing their people
- Keen to blame others
- Judgmental and temperamental
- Selfish
- Lacking in team/individual development
- Frequently defensive and insecure
- Dictatorial and autocratic
- Threatened by talent beneath them
- Take the credit for the good work of others
- Unwilling to allow their people access to higher authorities
- Unprofessional
- Manipulative and political

- Bad at providing positive feedback
- Practitioners of public humiliations
- Inconsistent
- Rude and bullying

Warning: why managers have traditionally got fired in organizations!

- Never delivered results
- Lacked a sense of urgency
- Lacked priorities
- Were unable to respond positively to change
- Clinged to obsolete ideas and outmoded ways of doing things
- Useless at managing people
- Emotionally volatile and unstable
- Immature in their behaviour towards others
- Gave up learning and developing themselves
- Were unable to delegate
- Ineffective communicator
- Unable to take tough decisions
- Lacked a sense of humour
- Lacked humility
- Failed to anticipate problems or challenges
- Focused more on 'I' rather than 'We'

CHAPTER TWO

Mastering yourself

Mastering yourself

Getting in shape for the future

Loyalty is a dead concept so start to get selfish.

As managers we have to clearly recognize – if we don't already know it, that we are living in very changing and challenging times and that the rate of change is continually accelerating. Security and comfort in our management roles is now a thing of the past. In today's knowledge era we must be totally focused on enhancing our own capability and market worth. This means we need a highly polished and prized set of up-to-date skills. Nowadays we never know when we might find ourselves in the wrong place at the wrong time. At the time of writing this book, a debate is taking place in economic and management circles as to whether job insecurity is any greater in the new millennium than it was ten years ago. Some commentators argue that it is not and that the job insecurity issue has been exaggerated. They argue that the so-called 'psychological contract' whereby employers and employees buy into the notion of fair pay and rewards for a fair day's work is alive and well. But, be it a hostile takeover or major downturn in market activity, I would argue that no one is safe in corporate life and that the traditional contract is now void. The fact is that organizations always have and always will pursue their own aims and objectives, and in the majority of instances this necessitates individual needs taking a back seat. No matter how successful or secure an organization is you can never be sure that some other organization will not acquire you, dramatically enter and destabilize your market or simply innovate you out of existence. We therefore need to think not so much about our job security but rather our employability.

So, I would argue that we have actually reached the stage where loyalty is an almost, if not already, outmoded concept for organizational and corporate life. There are no longer great prizes for staying with one employer for any great length of time as you leave yourself open to sudden changes which can catch you off guard. Moving from one employer to another used to be described as job hopping but today it is seen as a sign of someone who is taking care of their development. Of course there is nothing wrong with staying with one employer for a long time provided that you are growing and developing your skills and experience. The time to begin questioning this approach is when you sense that you are not developing.

So being selfish and managing your skill set and employability is a prerequisite of survival in today's corporate environment. The corporate world has never been a bigger jungle than it is today and taking action so as not to become another corporate victim is essential. If you ignore the need to develop your skill set, then you have only yourself to blame if events catch you out. The fact is we all need to get selfish and start thinking about our personal development in a big way. Remember, losing your job is no longer a capability issue – anyone can now find themselves in the wrong place at the wrong time. However, this is not meant to frighten but rather to alert people and provide a call to action. Although I suspect that for many people simply discussing this issue is deeply uncomfortable. But rather than avoid the issue we need to begin to get used to it and start to think about our skills and development as a long-term investment – after all it is our own research and development base and if we neglect it our overall value and worth falls.

Insecurity as a daily phenomenon

Remember – the only difference between a rut and a grave is the depth!

For most of us taking direct control and responsibility for our development is not an easy process to contemplate. Many of us work in large organizations because we perhaps feel we would be uncomfortable working in a smaller business or in a self-employed capacity. We may feel that we need the stimulus of an office environment to keep us motivated and that we would just not be able to plough our own way. The result is that we have not really been forced to think of alternatives or what would happen if we lost all the comforts (or what little remains) of our corporate life tomorrow. But the fact is that we now have to do so, and also be well prepared for it happening.

For those of us who want to start a process of continuous self improvement we may be a little uncertain about how to begin. If you have been working with one company for several years it is very easy to neglect your skills and knowledge development and also to forget how to market yourself. However, getting stuck in a rut and losing sight of your own brand image can be overcome with real determination and planning.

The starting point in enhancing your market value as an executive is to develop a personal brand plan that systematically sets targets and milestones to develop your skill set and capabilities.

Action plan

Getting in shape to deal with the uncertainty and job insecurity of today's world – the first step – think it could happen! But embrace the concept as a positive rather than a negative. See it as something that does not unduly threaten you because you have a positive view of your talents and capabilities.

Take the first step and start thinking and discussing the employability issue. Ask yourself:

- What would you do if you lost your job tomorrow?
- How much of a shock would it be?
- What would you plan to do?
- Have you developed any contingency plans?
- What would be your financial exposure? How long could you go before beginning to experience some discomfort?
- Do you have an up-to-date CV?
- What work or career avenues would be open to you?

The key point is to begin to confront the issue – to see it not as some traumatic event but as perhaps a normal feature of working in today's employment world. In many ways insecurity has always been there, it is just that in today's world it strikes without impunity and on a more widespread and frequent basis. The challenge therefore is to plan for it happening and not become a weak victim. Adopt a positive and aggressive approach to the challenge rather than a passive reactive one. The positive side of a more aggressive stance is that it also brings new opportunities and opens new doors.

Developing a personal brand plan – what is your brand value worth?

So start thinking about your own personal brand values. What is my asset base in terms of my experience, expertise and personal attributes? What do I offer any prospective organization? What is my Unique Selling Proposition (USP)?

A Personal Brand Plan (PBP) can help us to positively manage our working careers. Its purpose is to get us thinking in a structured way about our skills and market worth by committing to a process of continuous self-improvement – thereby enhancing our skills, experience and employability. It should also assist in guiding us towards greater job and work satisfaction.

A PBP assists us in realizing our full potential and worth through an ongoing process of knowledge, skills investment, development and review.

Getting focused – setting some personal objectives

When we have achieved a certain degree of success in our career and life's other commitments come along, such as partner's needs or children, we can naturally start to neglect our own needs and where we are going at work. In effect we can settle into a steady and comfortable routine – until of course that sudden crisis in the form of a merger or acquisition occurs and we start to worry about what happens next. Such crises galvanize us into late but very serious action to protect our future, either inside or outside the organization. A Personal Brand Plan forces us out of relaxed and complacent thinking, and challenges us to develop and manage our skills and capabilities on an ongoing basis.

The first step in any PBP involves setting some short, medium and long-term goals with regard to our work and private life. The purpose of any goal setting is to get us focused on what it is we really want to achieve in our business and work life. Of course this is not so easy as it first sounds. The question, **"What is it you want?"** is of course one of life's great challenges. Many of us spend our entire lives trying to find out what we want. Of course most people don't know what it is they really want in life or their work career. This most powerful of questions has an instant effect in getting someone to start people thinking about their future goals and ambitions. Being outcome-focused helps prevent us from drifting along. Setting clear goals helps to lift our thinking and provide a real focus for our day-to-day lives. Equally, the discipline of setting objectives and actually committing them to writing is a powerful process. If we leave things to chance the likelihood is that we will be disappointed. The mere act of writing down our key goals or outcomes can act as a constant reminder. Carrying our written goals around with us and reviewing them in either quiet or stressful moments can have an immediate impact in helping us to refocus our energies and thoughts.

We also need to think about the 'how' part of achieving any future outcomes. Wishful thinking alone is not enough to ensure success. We have to apply real effort and plan specific actions to get what we want. We need to be disciplined in questioning our current brand attributes. We may need to confront past failures as well as successes and we need to resolve what it is we want. So the starting point involves finding quality time to reflect on our future life and career ambitions and goals.

Answering these questions will help you start to develop your own Personal Brand Plan.

So start by reflecting on these fundamental questions:

- What is it I want from my job? Career? Life?
- How will I know I have got it? What would success look like?
- Am I happy with my present work role and career?
- Do I enjoy my working environment?
- Am I gaining the right level of financial reward for my efforts?
- Am I continuing to learn and develop?
- Have I continually had new challenges presented to me?
- Do I like working with my boss, colleagues, customers?
- Have I got the right balance between work and family?
- Does my role allow me the opportunity to pursue other interests outside of work? Have I already sacrificed certain things?
- What do I like doing? (At work or play.)
- Do I see an appropriate future beyond my existing role?
- Am I happy with any future developments as they might materialize?
- Is my current role stretching me as an individual?
- Am I satisfied with the investment being put into my development by myself and employer?
- Has my employer always delivered on promises?

Also in considering our work and personal goals we should ask what more do we want to achieve:

- A greater balance between career and home life?
- A more challenging working role?

- A better professional, academic or skills qualification?

- A change of organization or work role?

Drawing a life line chart

A simple and powerful way to review your current situation and reflect on the future is to draw what is called a career or life line. This is an intuitive process based on your own reflections and experiences that starts you looking at where you have been and what has worked and perhaps not worked so well for you. All you have to do is draw a line which reflects your life or career to date on the diagram illustrated below.

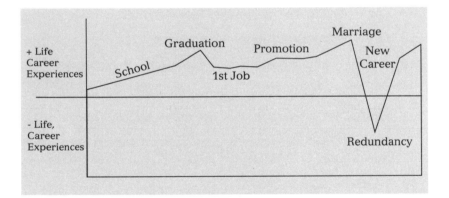

Anything above the line is a positive experience and below the line is regarded as a negative event. The height and depth of any points reflect your degree of delight or unhappiness with the event.

Begin the process by mapping out the big events in your life (school, sporting, academic success or failure, college, graduation, first jobs, marriage, children, divorce, career change, redundancy, promotion, birth, death of close ones etc).

Remember to leave space to fill in other events as certain experiences will trigger others.

Drawing your life line and reviewing these questions will help you to focus on the priorities to include in your Personal Brand Plan.

Once you have drawn your line reflect on the events and ask yourself some of the following questions. Using different signs to mark the events as you rate them:

- Which were the big positive experiences for me? Why were they so influential?
- What were the big lows? Why?
- From which experiences did I learn most?
- Where did I feel best suited and fulfilled?
- Where was I most under pressure or stressed?
- Where did I have most or least control? How did I feel about that?

Then consider the major themes that emerge from your life and career to date:

Ask yourself what are the common themes about the way you do things and the roles you seek out.

- What do you seem to value or prize most?
- What do you not like doing?

Have you engineered these changes yourself or have they happened by chance?

How much did luck play in your success?

Then consider your future:

- Where do you see yourself going in the future?
- What do you want to achieve?
- What would be your preferred role and personal circumstances?
- How is what you are doing today helping you to achieve what you really want?

Conducting a personal SWOT analysis

Another way of reviewing your future goals is to drawn up a personal SWOT analysis.

DEVELOPING A PERSONAL SWOT ANALYSIS

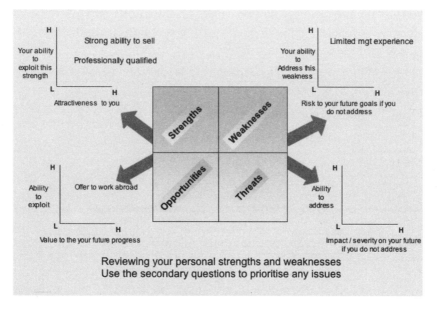

Reviewing your personal strengths and weaknesses
Use the secondary questions to prioritise any issues

Draw up your own personal SWOT analysis.

Many readers will know the SWOT technique – frequently used in strategy and planning exercises it can also be harnessed to assess an individual. A SWOT analysis asks us to list all our perceived strengths and weaknesses in terms of skills, attributes, interests, attitudes, likes and dislikes. At the same time we are asked to highlight any potential opportunities and threats that we may have to face. A SWOT analysis is very powerful for capturing on one sheet of paper our current capability and circumstances. Once we have exhausted our analysis we can then stand back and reflect on some critical issues, i.e. the things we really want to do or exploit, as well as highlighting the things we want to avoid.

Once we have reviewed our life/career line, developed a personal SWOT analysis and are clear on what we want to achieve, we can then start to set some objectives and key goals. When we set any personal objectives we always need to assess them against the acronym **SMART**: for any goal to be effective it must be:

Specific: Any goals should specify clear behaviour or actions.

Measurable: Our goals should specify a basis for measurement so that we know when they have been achieved.

Achievable: Goals should be within our capability to achieve.

Realistic: Any goal needs to be stretching but at the same time realistic.

Timely: Goals need to have a time element attached – when they will be achieved.

If any of our goals cannot be assessed against these five dimensions we should consider redrafting them. Whilst we can easily set goals without any real sense of commitment we need to remember that a personal brand plan requires us to be very disciplined. So we need to spend quality time to really focus on our key goals. We must be specific in terms of what we want to achieve and the timescales involved. We also need to ask ourselves if we are being realistic or unrealistic in our ambitions.

We should also consider who might help us in providing resources or encouragement to keep us on track when we inevitably lose interest. Indeed, having a close confident or colleague at work whom we implicitly trust can be a very valuable asset in helping us keep on track.

The seven essential questions in your personal brand plan

1   What new skills, capabilities or situations do you want to develop to enhance your value in your professional and/or personal life?

2   How do you intend to develop these skills and capabilities or engineer the right circumstances to acquire them – what are your specific plans?

3   What key activities or decisions will you need to undertake and by when?

4   What support will you need to achieve your goals?

5   What other information, resources or support will you need?

6   What key activities will you undertake and by when?

7   How and when will you review your progress?

Getting support for your personal brand plan (PBP)

The mentoring role

Having decided to develop a PBP and having mapped out a realistic action plan, we need to put our plan into action. Of course it is up to us as to how we go about it – but remember unless we do something... nothing will happen!!! All too often we fall short of committing ourselves to specific objectives and as a result time drifts and we find ourselves achieving very little. As we have already stated, the process of committing ourselves to pen and paper in drafting individual goals can be very powerful. So don't just think about it, DO IT TODAY and commit your goals to paper! You will find that it provides real focus and if you get into the habit of referring to them regularly they will help you stay focused and enable you to keep going even when you are feeling down.

Another means by which we can move forward on the personal development front is to make a contract with someone to help us over time. This does not need to be a formal or written arrangement but can be a simple verbal agreement with someone to act as a support or guiding source for your development plans. This supporting or facilitating role is often referred to as a mentor and it could be performed at work or outside by:

- A close colleague or friend.
- Your immediate manager.
- A group of colleagues.

A close colleague or friend

- Secure the support and advice of a close confident at work. This might be someone who has similar development plans or aspirations as yourself, or a friend who you trust a great deal. By working together and providing support and helpful advice and encouragement you can keep your energy up and maintain momentum to offset those difficult or stressful times when you might feel like giving up.

- When thinking about a mentor try to choose someone who:

    - already possesses some of the skills or capabilities you want to acquire so they can provide some form of help or advice immediately

    - will commit fully to helping you with support and encouragement – you in turn must also be willing to offer similar assistance if requested

    - you respect or admire in some way – someone who can be relied upon to listen at all times

    - you can fully trust and confide in.

Your immediate manager

If we have a successful working relationship with our manager there is no reason why we should not use them as a mentor. Good managers always play a strong mentoring or coaching role. Of course there may be occasions when we might want to be discrete about revealing long-term plans or ambitions with our immediate boss. Many of us might feel uncomfortable about talking about leaving our organization for another opportunity. Ultimately only you can decide if you feel comfortable in developing such a relationship with a boss. But certainly there are many managers who make great mentors and can provide excellent support. But choose carefully.

A group of colleagues

A small group of working colleagues can provide a wider network of support for carrying out the mentoring role, provided that everyone is fully committed to the process. Clearly a group working in such a way requires a strong sense of mutual respect and support. Trust, of course, is again integral to any such group. You have to be fully comfortable that confidences will be maintained and that there will be no betrayal of discussions outside of the group. This is clearly more challenging to put into place but with the right people you can do much to support each other and develop a strong network of mutual co-operation.

Whatever form of mentoring you select, you MUST commit to regularly review your development plan with your mentor. It is no use carrying out reviews in a haphazard manner. We must be disciplined to ensure that we are achieving the targets we have set ourselves. Recognize there will be times when you will not feel like doing it. It may be the workload is too heavy and stress levels are high but a continued commitment will pay off – remember at the end of the day it is your asset base that you are protecting.

Eight key activities to assist you in developing your asset base

1. Self-directed reading

Being aware of the brightest and best in your industry gives you power. If you can comment on your company or area of expertise then that is of value but, if you can also comment on what other competitors or industry sectors are doing then that gives you even more power, as it makes you more knowledgeable and useful to others. Ask yourself if you know enough about what is happening in your business, markets and industry. Self-directed reading is a process that involves developing your knowledge through a programme of targeted reading. To secure maximum benefit from the process we need to focus on the specific range and depth of information that we need to improve our knowledge base. When developing a programme of directed reading, consider the following sources to develop your knowledge and information database:

- Internal notes and minutes from key meetings.

- Internal reports and documents.

- Websites.

- In-house publications.

- Professional journals.

- Industry journals and websites.

- Books.

- Newspapers, magazines and periodicals.

Action points

- When reading be aggressive in making notes in the margin of books or underlining sections in articles and reports. Banish any childhood disciplines about not marking books etc – they are a resource: use them – but of course make sure you own them when you do this. Use highlighter pens to indicate important points or passages.

- If you see a good article in a newspaper or magazine about your business or interest area cut it out to read at a later date.

- Operate a binder where you put things to read for quiet periods.

2. Secondments

Secondments are concentrated periods of time spent in other departments or functions within your organization. The aim of a secondment is to help us understand how other parts of the organization operate. Alternatively, a secondment might take place with a customer or supplier to help us understand their businesses practices and approaches. If your organization does not operate such an approach why not ask or request that you spend some time working with another department, customer or supplier.

To achieve real benefit from any secondment establish:

- Clear objectives for the secondment period. What is it that you want to learn or develop?

- An agreed and structured programme of work – leaving things to the person we are allocated to is not advisable. So agree a set of clear learning objectives at the outset.

- A date for a structured review and follow up afterwards.

Report back the learning you have acquired to the business.

3. Training and development programmes

Training and development programmes when matched to our learning needs can provide an excellent and accelerated means of improving our skills and capabilities. When considering any training or development programme ask the following questions:

- What knowledge or skills do I want to improve or develop?
- Is a training programme the most effective way of meeting my needs? Can I gain the skills or knowledge by any other means?
- What courses are appropriate and available to obtain that knowledge or skill?
- What is the reputation of the course or provider?
- How will I evaluate the learning?
- What is it I want to emerge from the training being able to do?

4. DVDs

Another relatively easy and low cost option to develop our knowledge and skills are training and business DVDs. They offer a flexible resource which we can use in our own time. Today there are a vast array of DVDs covering almost every skill area. From interviewing skills to business and marketing strategies we can be sure that a product exists. Some organizations have developed their own DVD libraries so that people can help themselves and run the programme in their own time.

When using a DVD programme be sure to use any booklet which accompanies the programme to maximize the learning benefit.

5. Shadowing

Shadowing involves spending a period of time closely observing or accompanying people as they conduct their roles on a day-to-day basis. It might be regarded as similar to a secondment, but is generally more intensive and involves spending a much shorter period of time.

The aim of shadowing is to gain an understanding of a particular role or operating environment. Again, to secure maximum benefit from such an experience the person we shadow needs to have a clear understanding of what we want to achieve. At the same time they obviously need to be receptive to sharing information and insights on their role and work with us. Spending a day with a sales representative or engineer operating with customers in the market place can provide a valuable and interesting experience.

6. Coaching

Our everyday work provides valuable learning opportunities. Indeed, most of us actually learn more by working on the job. We can seek to maximize these learning opportunities through a structured process of coaching and guidance by selected managers. A coaching manager can provide extremely valuable sources of advice and guidance on a continuing basis.

7. Projects and assignments

Work projects and assignments can be powerful tools for learning and development, providing opportunities for developing skills in a number of key management activities including:

- Project design and management.
- Information gathering techniques.
- Interviewing skills.
- Problem solving skills.
- Analysis of information and generation of proposals.
- Report writing.
- Presentations.

As well as increasing our knowledge and skills, special projects or assignments also provide us with new information and insights into our organization. The important point when using this approach to aid your learning is to choose a project that involves a real live business issue. That way it will generate real management interest and so encourage us to generate a quality result and so heighten any learning experience.

Irrelevant projects which do not enjoy management interest are unlikely to motivate us to deliver superior results or outputs.

8. Open learning

Open learning is a process involving the acquisition of knowledge and skills at a pace and place determined by you and involving a range of learning media. It is an approach that has and will continue to grow very rapidly with the onset of new and more exciting forms of web-based media.

At the moment flexible learning revolves around one or more of the following medium or methods:

- Specially developed workbooks.
- Interactive DVDs.
- Learning manuals.
- Audio tapes.
- PC based learning – CD ROMs.
- The internet.
- Company IntraNets.

Clearly many people are benefiting from the continued explosion in opportunities via the Internet and in company IntraNets that enable people to download training and learning packages onto their work or home computers. The effect is to make your learning much more accessible.

Getting balanced – how to take control and manage yourself and your true value

1   Keep focused on your key goals. Don't be distracted from achieving those things that really matter to you.

2   Work smarter rather than harder. Don't confuse long hours with effectiveness or efficiency. Moving paper around does not create value. Focus on the urgent and important.

3   Avoid the use of negative internal dialogues such as 'I can't...' and 'Yes, But!!!' Stop saying 'I will try!' Instead say 'I will' – we often defeat ourselves before we begin. Choose your internal messages carefully – eradicate negative thoughts.

4   Avoid using words and expressions such as 'ought' and 'should have' – they infer feelings of guilt and anxiety. Instead use the words 'I could have' and 'I had the choice' – they are more liberating and neutral in their effect on you – they put you in control rather than make you feel guilty.

5   Make sure you are achieving the right balance between your personal and work life.

6   Develop your ability to manage stress. If necessary attend a training programme or read a book on stress management. Be clear as to what triggers stress in your role.

7   For each trigger develop coping strategies to manage them:

   • Stand back from the situation and find time to collect your thoughts and response.

   • Change or avoid the situations you find stressful.

   • Change your internal response to the stress trigger 'I will no longer allow myself to react in that way!'

- Change your working hours – begin work earlier and finish earlier.

- Vary your breaks during the day – take time out to refresh yourself – particularly when the pressure is on.

- Stay fit by exercising regularly – 20 minutes a day is all it takes.

8   Learn to relax and take time out for yourself. Reward yourself and do something that you enjoy – playing sport or some other hobby.

9   Avoid work becoming routine or a 'chore' vary your routine and do something different on a regular basis – seek out new experiences.

10 Keep a record of your regular work tasks. Prioritize those tasks that are critical. Ask yourself whether you are getting the best results in these areas? Stay focused on the vital few and avoid trying to do everything.

11 Review the decisions you make over a couple of weeks and analyze how much time you devote to each one. Are you spending sufficient time on the important things?

12 When making decisions ask yourself either the cost of getting it wrong or the benefit of getting it right. Allocate sufficient time based on your answer.

13 Operate a daily mental 'development diary'. At the end of each day ask yourself:

- What did I learn today?

- What have I done that was new?

- What have I accomplished?

- What must I do tomorrow?

14 Say "NO" to people who place unreasonable demands on you.

15 Make telephone calls rather than spend time writing long e-mails and letters.

16 Try to reduce the length of all your written communications –
    e-mails, letters, minutes, memos, reports, instructions by 50%.

17 Seek out opportunities to make presentations and develop your
    skills in this vital business area.

18 Ask close friends to give you real feedback on your perform-
    ance during meetings, presentations etc.

19 In preparing for a difficult interview, presentation or negotia-
    tion, practice or role play it with a close colleague. Get their
    reactions to your proposed approach.

20 After attending any training programme make sure you review
    your notes within a week of your return, make a record of any
    points that you regard as especially important and that you will
    apply in your organization. Produce a short report for your
    manager – better still make a presentation to the management
    team on some recommendations that the business should
    consider taking.

Assess your management skills

Personal development questionnaire

This questionnaire is designed to help you start thinking about your
personal development at work. It highlights some of the classic skill areas
in managing and leading people.

- Review the list of skills below and decide which of the areas are
  important to your personal development.

- As the list of skills and competences is not meant to be exhaus-
  tive you should add others if you feel they are appropriate.

- At the end of the questionnaire identify the critical areas that
  you need to develop and consider some plans for developing
  those skills.

General management skills and competences	I'm doing OK	I need to do more	I need to do less
1 Thinking before I speak			
2 Communicating effectively with my team			
3 Being brief and concise when communicating			
4 Putting forward my points of view to others			
5 Making presentations to a group or team			
6 Developing other people's contributions			
7 Reading the organization's politics			
8 Being assertive with others			
9 Listening to other people			
10 Contributing fully at meetings			
11 Using effective writing skills			
12 Understanding team dynamics			
13 Recognizing and resolving conflicts in my team			
14 Recognizing who needs support in my team			
15 Spotting talent and potential in others			

General management skills and competences	I'm doing OK	I need to do more	I need to do less
16 Being ruthless in dealing with paperwork			
17 Managing my time effectively			
18 Planning my day at the beginning			
19 Being attentive to detail			
20 Being creative and innovative			
21 Seeking out more challenges and responsibility			
22 Focusing on my priorities			
23 Preventing interruptions to my work plans			
24 Delegating unimportant tasks			
25 Finding time to reflect on the 'big picture'			
26 Understanding other people's role(s)			
27 Developing strong team spirit			
28 Showing interest in other people's needs			
29 Displaying trust in others			
30 Motivating others			

General management skills and competences	I'm doing OK	I need to do more	I need to do less
31 Challenging people's ideas and assumptions			
32 Giving positive feedback and recognition			
33 Coaching, training and developing individuals			
34 Establishing an atmosphere of trust in my team			
35 Leading my team in an effective style			
36 Encouraging team involvement in decision making			
37 Communicating to others what I want			
38 Understanding and managing change			
39 Helping to sell changes			
40 Recognizing when people are under stress			
41 Managing others who are under pressure			
42 Disagreeing openly with others			
43 Encouraging others to challenge my ideas			
44 Highlighting problems or challenges in plans or proposals			

General management skills and competences	I'm doing OK	I need to do more	I need to do less
45 Trusting others to do things			
46 Being a good coach to my people			
47 Assessing risk in situations			
48 Managing stress and being relaxed when under pressure			
49 Dealing with conflicts			
50 Resolving differences between others			
51 Dealing with a lack of co-operation from others			
52 Facing up to disappointments			
53 Being comfortable with asking for help when I need it			
54 Handling difficult clients/customers			
55 Meeting with customers and clients			
56 Offering advice on training and career development to my people			
57 Understanding other people's values			
58 Keeping up-to-date with the latest developments in my field of expertise			

General management skills and competences	I'm doing OK	I need to do more	I need to do less
59 Understanding our management information systems			
60 Increasing my under-standing and use of Information Technology			
61 Understanding and managing my responsibili-ties in disciplinary and grievance procedures			
62 Asking for feedback on my performance			
63 Asking for ideas/opinions from my peers			
64 Analyzing problems and their real causes			
65 Confronting problems in the organization			
66 Understanding the needs of other units that I have to work with			
67 Identifying and managing my career options			

Identify areas for development at work

List here the skills and competences that you think you need to be developing as a priority. What plans can you make to ensure that you will begin to acquire these skills?

Try to be specific and commit to some real actions with timescales.

Skills and competences I want to develop

1

Time scale:

2

Time scale:

3

Time scale:

4

Time scale:

5

Time scale:

6

Time scale:

7

Time scale:

8

Time scale:

CHAPTER THREE

Mastering performance management

Mastering performance management

Managing performance

All of us want more than money from our work. We want roles that are interesting, challenging, and developmental. Most of us also want to participate in the process of setting and agreeing our work objectives. These are essential elements to working in a stimulating work environment. Any process of managing performance must involve managers in a continuous and ongoing discussion with every member of the team. This process, which is often called Performance Management, is a structured approach to ensuring that we get the important things done. It is a way of clarifying:

- What your organization and boss expect from you.

- The respective roles of the manager and individual team members.

- Your training and development needs.

Things to avoid in implementing any performance management process

Many organizations have introduced performance management processes or systems. Whilst many work well, a lot more fall into disrepair. Some of the most common pitfalls to beset the performance management process include:

- **An over reliance on procedures and paper** – do not allow your system to become too complex. Lengthy forms and numerous 'signing off' procedures do not encourage managers to use the system. Restrict any documentation to no more than two pages and keep your overall approach simple.

- **Poorly trained managers** – conducting a structured and open discussion about performance requires critical skills in active listening and giving feedback. Make sure managers are trained effectively and know how to not only give advice but also to listen. There is a big difference between giving advice and coaching and counselling people!

- **Poorly defined targets** – any performance management process must deliver an agreed set of objectives and targets between managers and staff. If the process fails to deliver these critical outputs it will soon fail.

- **Lack of management commitment** – if the process fails to enjoy the full support of management then it will be seen as a passing fad and managers will relegate it down their list of priorities. Make sure your system has the full and visible support of senior management.

- **Lack of sanctions for non-completion** – if managers are not incentivized or penalized for completing the performance management process you will get flawed implementation. Link elements of your bonuses and pay rises to the completion of performance management discussions – that way you'll ensure they are done in a timely manner.

Motivating people at work also involves improving the team's performance, and any performance management process must be applied on a consistent basis across all team members to gain maximum benefit. A classic process for managing performance is illustrated below. In our earlier management model of empowering, enabling and reviewing we referred to this approach which highlights the essential elements that managers need to follow.

Agreeing the purpose of the role

It is essential that the manager and individual team members understand and agree their respective roles. This agreed definition and purpose can only be achieved by a focused discussion. People have to know why their roles exist and what their key outcomes in terms of performance and delivery are. Most people will, of course, want to have a discussion about any goals that they are being asked to deliver. Some organizations describe these goals as Key Result Areas or KRAs. These spell out the detailed results that need to be achieved by the individual.

What are Key Results Areas – KRAs?

There are generally four types of KRA:

1   Operational KRAs – these consist of your essential core performance indicators. The critical business measures that must be delivered.

2   Projects – these are specific 'one off' pieces of work that have been allocated to your role.

3   Personal development – these are targets that might be set as part of your ongoing self development, e.g. professional development.

4   People development – these are targets set around the development of any staff you might have.

Setting individual objectives and establishing commitment

As managers we can clearly demonstrate confidence in people by involving them in any objective setting process. This is likely to increase levels of commitment to achieving any agreed goals. The words we use as managers are the most powerful resources we have in terms of developing confidence in others. In agreeing performance standards and KRAs we have to successfully coach performance and in so doing employ the critical people skills of:

- *Active listening.*

- *Questioning.*

- *Giving and receiving feedback – both positive and negative.*

SO WHAT IS AN OBJECTIVE?

An objective is a statement of what tasks have to be completed and the measures by which it will be judged to have been successfully accomplished. An objective therefore makes a statement of:

- What needs to be done.

- Why it needs to be done.

- When it needs to be done by – time.

- The quality with which it needs to be done – standards required in terms of cost and quality.

How to develop effective objectives

When setting objectives and assessing the ability of an individual to complete a task ask yourself these two fundamental questions:

How competent is the individual to carry out the task?

How committed and motivated is the individual to carry out the task?

Your responses to these two questions will provide you with a quick assessment of what you need to do in providing the necessary level of direction and control to the individual. We might catagorize the various responses into four distinct types of capability:

- **Competent and committed** people are self motivated. The chances are that you can let this person get on with minimal supervison and direction. These people are self-starters and will want to be stretched and respond well to being empowered. They will react favourably towards being set challenging targets and objectives.

- **Committed but not yet competent (still learning).** These people can be stretched but not excessively as their lack of competence means you will have to provide an appropriate level of coaching support and guidance around the task side of their work. But if shown how to do things they will pick it up and work to deliver performance through the application of their high level of motivation. They want to succeed. But be careful as setting unrealistic targets with this individual might easily destroy their developing confidence. You need to explain what needs to be done and then help them to get to a level of capability before letting go.

- **Competent but not committed.** If someone is not committed to their role but are considered competent in carrying it out you will need to find out what the real problem is. This individual will almost certainly require some kind of counselling discussion. It could be that the person is simply bored and no longer stimulated by the role. Equally they might have some other private issues that are getting in the way of their work role. Either way you need to find out what their thinking is as they are obviously capable of greater performance but until you can resolve the motivation issue their performance will be sub-optimal

- **Incompetent and uncommitted.** This is clearly a problem individual and so will require a concerted approach to find out what the underlying problem is. You will need to identify whether it is a training, personal or competence issue or possibly a complex combination of all three. This type of individual can absorb a lot of management time and so requires swift and decisive management attention. You cannot afford to waste too much time with this level of capability so prompt action is vital.

BE OUTCOME FOCUSED AND USE PERFORMANCE MEASURES

When setting any objectives think outcomes. Make sure objectives are stated in a way that emphasizes a clear set of outputs. Remember an outcome might be a specific and measurable result, service, or behaviour. For example, an increase in sales of 10% by the third quarter or a reduction in individual customer response times from 30 to 15 minutes within the next two months.

A performance measure sets out how someone will know whether they have achieved their objective(s) or not. Performance indicators often refer to:

- Time (the 'by when' criteria).

- Quantity (how many will be produced, sold, delivered, saved, transferred).

- Quality (the level of satisfaction to be reached or attained).

THE NEED TO 'BUILD-IN' PERFORMANCE STANDARDS

Good objectives always have an explicit performance standard built into the task activity. For example, to increase the sales of product X by 25% by the end of Quarter 1. In activities where it is not immediately apparent what the performance standard or outcome is, you may need to work harder to build in a clear performance standard to avoid any ambiguity. For example, 'To regularly update the customer database.' Such an objective is too loose and would benefit by the addition of more specific performance indicators. So it could be rewritten to include the following:

> 'To update the customer database by 16:00 on Friday of each week and to transfer that data onto the main company database at each month end.'

This ensures that both the manager and team member are absolutely clear what is required in terms of deliverables.

When developing objectives we also have to focus on some additional questions:

- What levels of desired performance can be achieved?

- Is the person or team working as effectively as possible to achieve these objectives?

- Are there other ways by which we can improve performance?

USE ACTION WORDS WHEN SHAPING OBJECTIVES AND OUTCOMES

Make sure your objectives include a precise and appropriate action verb to articulate what someone has to do. Such words provide a bias towards action and again focuses thoughts and energies. Consider for example:

Construct, develop, produce, analyze, detect, reduce, complete, deliver, prepare, update, develop, introduce, deliver, reorganize, promote, build, set up, achieve, increase, generate, expand, reduce.

Monitoring performance

In order for people to understand how they are performing, managers also have to provide timely feedback on performance. Any feedback provided should be based on the agreed objectives and performance standards. Only by regularly monitoring individual performance can we measure real effectiveness. This practice also provides a framework for the discussion of individual strengths and weaknesses in relation to performance. Through the use of regular reviews we can motivate staff to consistently increase performance and encourage them to monitor their own performance.

Management warning: Whilst performance might improve as a result of aggressive behaviour such as threats and intimidation, any improvement is only ever likely to be short-lived. Bullying managers who impose unrealistic objectives will invariably come up losers – even if it takes a rather long time for any backlash to occur. At the same time, in today's litigation minded culture, the era of the bullying manager is coming to an end as corporate leaders recognize the legal implications of allowing staff to be bullied by unscrupulous managers.

Evaluating performance

Evaluating performance is a critical element of any performance management process. Without it the whole cycle collapses. Evaluating performance allows you to check the endeavours of your team members and to reward high performance. As well as also dealing with poor performance, it also helps you to identify any factors that may have been outside of someone's control and so adversely affected their results.

The evaluation process also enables you to reset the goals and so resume the performance management process.

Objective setting checklist

		YES	NO
1	I regularly discuss and agree objectives and KRAs with my people.	☐	☐
2	I hold regular (monthly) performance discussions.	☐	☐
3	I focus on a maximum of six key objectives or KRAs.	☐	☐
4	Clear performance measures are always agreed.	☐	☐
5	Any objectives set are realistic and achievable.	☐	☐
6	Objectives are agreed through discussion rather than management dictate.	☐	☐
7	Objectives are revised in the light of any major external changes.	☐	☐
8	People are provided with all the necessary resources to carry out their work.	☐	☐
9	People can access me to get any additional support or guidance should they need it.	☐	☐
	Total	☐	☐

Influencing people

The performance management process obviously requires a high degree of influencing skills to achieve positive results. It may be easy to tell someone what they have to achieve in a classic authoritarian style, but to motivate someone to work towards a set of self-defined objectives requires a higher and more mature level of people skills.

It is sometimes assumed that influencing skills, like leadership skills, are a gift that some people are born with. This might be true for a very small majority but it is not true for the vast majority of managers as we are all capable of improving our skills in influencing and persuading others. What we have to recognize is that in order to influence others we need to first understand what motivates and drives them. We often get into difficulties managing other people because we assume that they are motivated by exactly the same things. This is of course a big mistake as people generally do things for their own reasons and motivations, not ours. In seeking to influence others we also need to realize the impact of different influencing strategies.

Many of us, because of our life and work experiences, tend to develop a relatively narrow range of influencing strategies that we apply to all our work situations. In order to become truly successful influencers of people we need to develop far greater flexiblity in matching our influencing styles to particular people and situations. An understanding of the classic influencing styles can therefore help us begin to review our own approach and strategies.

Before using any influencing style we firstly need to be very clear on the outcomes we want to achieve. We then need to analyze the exact situation we are facing and then seek to recognize the other person's perspective. A little advance planning and thought before we jump into situations can pay real dividends in helping us develop appropriate responses. Perhaps the most important thing to do when trying to influence others is to listen to what the other person is saying and seek to really understand their position and needs. Too often we allow our own needs to dominate and so lose sight of other strategies that might be employed in trying to move people to another position.

Some basic influencing styles – their strengths and downsides

Influencing style/use of	Strengths	Possible downside
Logic and data analysis	Ensures no detail is missed	Can be seen as too precise and controlled – loses out on spontaneity.
"The facts of the matter are"	Focuses on facts and data	May be dismissive of emotional issues and clues which could lie at the root of the problem.
Aggressive/ critical	High energy	May result in an aggressive and negative response. "I Win v.You Lose" perspectives. Too direct and blunt in approach for some.
"This report is rubbish"	Provides release for the giver	Often lacks precision in terms of what is said. Liable to escalate matters.
Use of status	Uses formal authority and executive power	People may either comply, become dependent, or rebel.
"I'm the boss here"	Easy to apply – I am the boss and therefore I expect...	Excessive and long-term use might generate sub-optimal results. Resentment and sabotage can soon follow.
Friendship and empathy	Develops friendly relationships and builds strong team spirit	If not done might well be viewed as insincere or even manipulative.
"Could you do me a favour please?"	Easy to appeal to	May be less effective when tough decisions have to be made. If overdone might be viewed as a sign of weakness by others.

Influencing style/use of	Strengths	Possible downside
Supportive approach	Encourages individuals. Builds on their ideas.	May be seen as taking sides or having favourites.
"We can both benefit"	"Can I help or support you on that…"– helps build networks and alliances.	Possible downside might be felt to provide no direction or guidance.
Listening/ questioning to obtain opinions/ views	People feel their ideas are valued	May cause anxiety if the questioning is too tough or persistent.
"What are your views"	Leads to a full understanding	Has to be supported by commitment and action otherwise constant questioning may cause irritation.
Being open and revealing oneself	Projects honesty which may facilitate full understanding.	Can be seen by some as overly emotional and lacking in 'professionalism' too 'touchy feely'.
"Can I be honest with you"	Promotes high levels of trust	May result in a "Let's stick to the facts!" type response – not rational enough!

Classic influencing styles in detail

The following builds on the approaches highlighted above and illustrate some of the most commonly employed influencing styles used in normal business life. When reviewing these styles reflect on your own influencing strategies and consider whether or not you need to develop or add to your range of styles. In order to be effective we need to be able to call upon a range of styles and employ them in appropriate circumstances. In any influencing situation it is the person who possesses the greatest flexibility in a range of styles who will ultimately succeed. If we get stuck into one pattern we might win sometimes but we will also have our fair share of failures.

- **Stating your own position** – being assertive.

- **Intuitive/creative** – gut feel, hunches.

- **Logical** – the facts.

- **Supportive** – developing a common agenda.

- **Judgmental** – discriminating/criticizing.

- **Clarifying the position of others** – developing an understanding.

Stating your own position – being assertive – the characteristics

- Being persistent about your own needs and requirements.

- Declaring your needs and wants.

- Stating your rights – "I am entitled to X".

- Being strong without damaging others.

- Demanding from other people.

STATEMENTS

- I appreciate your point but I must again request the following…

- I want to make it clear to you that I expect…

- I feel you have not understood my position so let me again reiterate it…

- I need to know that you have ensured the following…

- My situation is such that I am not prepared to accept that response because…

- My concern is…

- That proposal gives me a problem because I want to…

Intuitive/creative – the characteristics

- Proposing new ideas.

- Raising alternative approaches.

- Brainstorming radical methods.

- Challenging others' methods, thinking and assumptions.

- I suggest we tackle this from a different angle.

- How about looking at the situation from another perspective.

- Here's a new idea.

- What would happen if we did...?

- Shouldn't we really be focusing on...?

- I really feel that we should be looking at some more radical alternatives...

- What if...?

- Aren't we missing the point here! Surely we need to focus on x not y...!

Logical – the characteristics

- Stating the facts – using the data and evidence.

- Keeping things to the point.

- Being rational and calm.

- Applying logic and analysis.

- Evaluating the criteria.

STATEMENTS

- Let's look at the facts as they really are.

- Simply look at the reality of the situation.

- That is simply not supported by the figures.

- The evidence does not support that approach.

- We really need to focus on the data and the reality of the results.

- We should really keep those judgmental and emotive issues outside of the discussion.

- That is not logical.

- That idea would never work because of...

- Where is your evidence?

- How can you justify or support that argument or approach? I see no evidence for it in the data?

Supportive – the characteristics

- Involving and bringing in other people.

- Rewarding others for their contributions and efforts.

- Building on others' ideas.

- Offering positive ideas and suggestions to build on other contributions.

STATEMENTS

- I understand how you feel.

- That's an excellent idea.

- I fully appreciate your situation.

- That could prove an important issue that Max has just mentioned, perhaps we should discuss it in more detail.

- I like the way you outlined the challenge.

- What if we thought about the point raised by Jean.

- I found that a helpful input on the problem.

- If we also added x to your suggestion that might also help.

Judgmental – the characteristics

- Being overly critical.
- Disagreeing.
- Highlighting obstacles.
- Seeing only problems.

- I disagree...
- That will not work because of...
- That's rubbish!
- You seem to have missed several key points.
- You have overlooked the problem of xyz.
- Yes, but...
- We seem to have a major disagreement here.
- This is getting us nowhere – you are clearly failing to see the problem.
- Your analysis is overly simplistic.
- That's a preposterous idea.

Clarifying others' positions – the characteristics

- Drawing out other people's ideas.
- Probing for more information.
- Seeking more facts.
- Listening, showing understanding.
- Picking up unspoken feelings, non-verbal cues.

- Could you say more about that?
- What do you need to say?
- Can you give an example?
- You sound as though you have more to say about that issue?

- To sum up what you are saying...

- Could I check I have fully understood what you are saying?

- It sounds like you really feel/think that.

- I sense you are not very pleased about the issue. Is that true?

- Have I understood what you have said correctly? You are saying the following...

What influencing styles do you use?

- Do you have the right range and balance of styles?

- Do you use too much of any style? What is the consequence of that?

- What styles do you find it difficult to deal with? Why? How could you learn to cope with them?

- What other styles do you need to develop to become more effective?

- Generate a list of new influencing statements or expressions that you could practise using in meetings or in other influencing type situations.

Using power to influence others – where do you get yours from?

In the corporate world we normally associate power with the level of executive authority someone possesses. Yet the authority we get in an organization is not always simply a function of our position or rank. The fact is that there are many other sources of authority that we can potentially use to influence colleagues. Consider which ones you use and ask yourself how would you manage if you lost your current sources of power tomorrow. How would you get things done?

Hierarchical   This is the power you derive based on your position in your management or organization structure. It is the source of power that most people rely on.

Information	Power that comes from having information or knowledge that others do not possess – for example your access to specific technical or market knowledge.
Expertise	Possessing a particular skill set or range of experiences that others do not.
Reputation	The power you gain from your proven track record and past performance. "They always deliver the results!" "She knows what she is talking about!"
Charisma	The magic ingredient – personality, voice, appearance, energy, warmth, presence etc. Often very difficult to define but easy to identify.
Positional	This power comes from the unique nature of your role, e.g. being in a key position in a critical communication network – close to the customer or the problem.
Coercive	The power to punish and impose sanctions on others. Possibly linked to hierarchical power.

Ineffective managers will tend to rely on one or two sources of power to get things done, normally hierarchical and positional. Conversely, effective managers will operate from several power bases. In an increasingly knowledge-based work environment we cannot simply rely on the power that comes to us from our position. Increasingly we see a greater emphasis being placed on expertise and knowledge as the key sources of influence and power. Consequently we will all need to develop other sources of power in order to influence people successfully.

To influence someone successfully we need to analyze the situation and the type of person we are dealing with. We need to reflect on the level of authority people possess and their desired aims and objectives as well as our own. We then have to be able to employ a range of influencing styles based on our interpretation of all these factors. In so doing we have to avoid falling into the trap of relying on one approach and so antagonizing the other person. Only by being aware of our own natural preferences and the alternative approaches is it possible to identify and select the most effective strategy to influence others. Ultimately it is all about the words we use and how we say them.

Effective delegation

Most managers complain of an excessive workload with too much to do in too little time. Learning to delegate is therefore one of the the most vital skills of all to master. Effective delegation can then help to bring relief to a demanding and heavy workload, and also help develop other team members. In order to delegate effectively we first need to reflect on and be able to identify which of the huge number of our daily work tasks could actually be performed by other members of our team.

Before delegating any activity or task we need to consider two critical dimensions: the **importance** and **urgency** of the task.

The diagram below illustrates a simple but powerful matrix that can help us decide whether we should be holding onto a task or activity or delegating it to someone else.

The Urgency and Importance grid

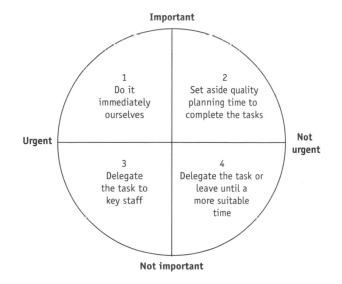

1   If a task is both urgent and important then we should complete it ourselves, as quickly as possible.

2   If a task is not particularly urgent but it is important, we can either complete the task ourselves or delegate parts of it to team members. In most cases we need to set aside quality time to deal with this task

3   If a task is urgent but not important it is probably most effectively tackled by some other member of the team.

4   A task that is neither important nor urgent can be left until you delegate someone else to deal with it.

The matrix provides an easy and practical approach to thinking about our workload. Having decided that a task needs to be delegated, we then need to use our managing performance skills for allocating the task to a team member. In so doing we need to be clear as to the standard of work required and the requisite timescales and quality standards. We then have to ensure we have a simple but effective follow-up process to monitor the completion of the task. If we don't apply our performance management skills we may be simply 'dumping' tasks on people. We also have to remember to use the situational approach which urges us to consider the two questions of a person's ability and motivation to complete a task.

Am I delegating enough? A simple checklist

Answer these questions with a yes or no response. It will help you think about whether or not you need to be improving your skills in delegating.

		YES	NO
1	I find it difficult to delegate important tasks or work.	☐	☐
2	My team complain that they sometimes have insufficient work to do.	☐	☐
3	Team members seem to feel there is not enough challenge in their work.	☐	☐
4	I frequently believe that my team is less effective than me.	☐	☐
5	I often do tasks myself, as I find it not only quicker but that it also produces a better result.	☐	☐
6	I rarely ask myself 'Should I really be doing this?' as I know I can do it faster and to a higher standard.	☐	☐
7	I do not allow people to make mistakes.	☐	☐
8	I explain precisely how any task or piece of work should be carried out.	☐	☐
9	I tend to work longer hours than my team.	☐	☐
10	I do not have the time to train and develop my team.	☐	☐
	Total	☐	☐

A process for managing delegation is outlined in the flow chart below:

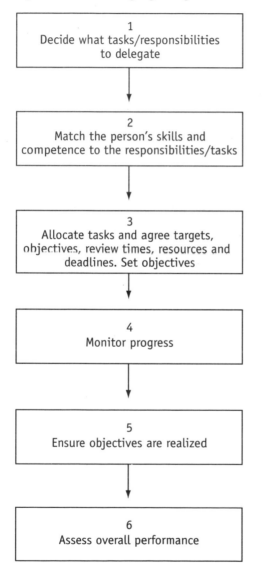

```
┌─────────────────────────────────────┐
│                  1                   │
│    Decide what tasks/responsibilities│
│              to delegate             │
└─────────────────────────────────────┘
                   │
                   ▼
┌─────────────────────────────────────┐
│                  2                   │
│      Match the person's skills and   │
│  competence to the responsibilities/tasks│
└─────────────────────────────────────┘
                   │
                   ▼
┌─────────────────────────────────────┐
│                  3                   │
│    Allocate tasks and agree targets, │
│ objectives, review times, resources and│
│         deadlines. Set objectives    │
└─────────────────────────────────────┘
                   │
                   ▼
┌─────────────────────────────────────┐
│                  4                   │
│           Monitor progress           │
└─────────────────────────────────────┘
                   │
                   ▼
┌─────────────────────────────────────┐
│                  5                   │
│      Ensure objectives are realized  │
└─────────────────────────────────────┘
                   │
                   ▼
┌─────────────────────────────────────┐
│                  6                   │
│      Assess overall performance      │
└─────────────────────────────────────┘
```

Am I the most suitable person to be doing this task?

CHAPTER FOUR

Mastering face-to-face communications

Mastering face-to-face communications

Effective communications skills and capabilities lie at the heart of any successful business or organization. No matter how good your plans or strategies are, if you fail to communicate them you will not achieve success. Every leader needs to be an accomplished communicator in order to thrive and enjoy real commitment from their people. But the fact is that when it comes to communicating most of us might be good at telling people what we want but all too often we are not good at listening. When we are faced with difficult situations or under stress *we frequently hear but fail to listen* and there is a huge difference between the two capabilities. In our day-to-day work we are receiving information all the time – through written reports, facts, figures, and in meetings and presentations. Most of the information we receive can of course be interpreted in all manner of ways. We often interpret information with reference to our past experiences and what interests us, so we have a unique perception of what is happening during a presentation or around a meeting table. Ultimately, how we respond to information will depend upon our interpretation of it as we have received it. When we receive information we often filter it based on lots of influences such as past experiences or assumptions we have developed. For example, if I decide that all lawyers cannot be trusted (because of some past negative experience) I may find that I am always negative in any interaction with them. If we extend such behaviours to other functions or areas of activity (e.g. production people never want to help sales) we have a real minefield of communication problems between people. This is exactly what does happen in large organizations – sales argue with marketing, technical people argue with sales and the production department doesn't get on with marketing, and so it goes on. So these filters and negative judgements all help to distort our ability to listen. This creates bias, confusion and in some instances conflict.

Other factors that limit our capacity for listening include:

- Too much information coming in – we experience overload!
- Information that is too complex to digest – we simply don't have the ability to absorb it.
- We are not interested in the information we receive.
- We disagree with the information we are receiving.
- We don't like the person giving the message or information.
- We ignore the real message and hear what we want to hear.

These factors frequently mean that we tune out and switch off! So one of the simplest and most powerful ways to improve our influencing and general communications skills is to become a better listener. As with other management skills this is a learnt behaviour and relates to our effectiveness rather than our innate personality: so we can all become better listeners if we practise.

How to really listen

Real listening involves active listening and this means demonstrating that we are interested not only in the content of what is being said, but also the context of the discussion and the feelings being expressed by the speaker. This process involves 'making sense' of what we have heard. It also involves the potentially dangerous application of selective hearing, whereby our existing assumptions or 'mental models' influence our responses to any information we receive. When we apply selective hearing we only notice elements of what has been said or not said. In effect, we listen to what we want to hear, whether it has been said or not. This often results in misunderstandings and conflicts as we distort the real message that might have been given to us. Selective interpretation is also supported by a process that involves us evaluating the information. So even when we do hear accurately what has been said and are able to make sense of it, we frequently subject the information or message to our own values and prejudices. Thus it is very easy to allow our feelings to influence the weighting or interpretation we give to any message or information we receive.

We only need to think of our personal relationships to see the impact and power of this process. Parents and children often clash because of selective interpretation. "I asked them not to come home too late and they thought I was criticizing them for being irresponsible, when all I did was ask them not to come home late!"

Six fundamental questions to ask yourself to improve your communications style

What am I trying to say? Know your outcome!

Make sure you are clear about the information or message you are trying to convey. Practise an outcome focused approach. What is it you want to say? Are you clear? When communicating be precise and succinct. Remember, fewer words are better than too many.

What impact do I want to create on other people?

Make sure the words you choose are going to support your message. Are your words reflecting the message you want to give? Think anger, control, logic, mature, passion etc – be clear about what you want to achieve from your message – a reaction, agreement or a decision?

Am I sticking to the facts?

Make sure the information you are providing is accurate and not unduly influenced too much by a personal agenda – unless a technical opinion or some form of personal disclosure is essential to helping you achieve your objective. In cases where you want people to act, remember that they may only be able to make a decision if they have all the facts. Check whether you are providing the facts to help them understand your position or argument.

Can I deliver on my commitments?

When faced with difficult or time pressurized situations we might be tempted to promise something to win people over to our side of an argument. But remember that any subsequent failure to deliver on hard promises given will generate real disappointment and ultimately erode trust – and trust is one of the fundamentals of good communication. So if you are providing any commitments remember that you must be committed to deliver them.

Am I prepared to follow up?

In any effective working relationship effective communications must be an ongoing process and not an isolated or intermittent activity. So be prepared to answer or follow up on any questions or issues that might have been raised with you. Learn to accept questions and queries as feedback and commit to dealing with them.

Am I consistent and credible?

If you are new to a management position then a degree of distance from your team can often result. In some instances it may be a good thing to keep a certain distance, after all you are now the boss and some people will view you differently. But at all times be consistent and honest in your communications with people. Stick to your commitments and avoid double dealing. Be fair and credible in your communications and you will find that trust will follow.

Remember we all have a tremendous capacity to receive messages in different ways. We are all influenced by personalities, values, and assumptions. So take time to check out that people have really understood what you have communicated. With flatter and more matrix type corporate structures effective communication is more important than ever. It is vital that we get it right and ensure that we communicate and listen with equal measure.

Communications checklist

When communicating with others do:

- Make strong eye contact – it demonstrates trust, honesty and shows interest. Try to identify the colour of peoples' eyes at a first contact or handshake. But avoid staring as that is threatening. A failure to make eye contact can lead people to make lots of assumptions about you, e.g. he is shy, lacks confidence, is arrogant or even lying etc etc – all from a failure to connect the eyes.

- Check your understanding of what has been said by summarizing, paraphrasing or reflecting back to the speaker. Use expressions such as, *"If I have understood you correctly you are saying the system cannot work because of x – have I understood you correctly?"* This is a critical skill to becoming a good listener.

- Make sure your body language and tone of voice reflect genuine interest – try leaning towards the speaker and responding with a questioning or reflective tone of voice. Avoid negative or distant body language if you want to show a real interest.

- Convey enthusiasm in your voice when necessary – adjusting your physiology – the way you are sitting or standing can very easily adjust your vocal tone.

- Listen for any feelings as well as facts in what is being said. Some of us only listen for the facts or data – which may account for only 20% of the problem or issue. Try to pick up any emotional element to the speaker – are they passionate or angry?

When communicating don't:

- Interrupt the other person as they are talking.

- Finish off the end of their sentences.

- Let your mind wander during the discussion.

- Spend listening time thinking about your next question – focus on the speaker and what they are saying.

- Focus on just one element of the discussion and miss the main part of the message.

Remember the facts about communication

- About 80% of our waking hours are spent communicating. We spend approximately 45% of this time listening.

- In meetings we tend to spend about 60-70% of our time listening.

- After a ten minute presentation we only hear, understand, evaluate and retain approximately 50% of what is said. After 48 hours this can fall to as little as 25%.

- Remember, our listening habits are not the result of training but rather the lack of it.

Listening and communicating to others – some basic rules

There are a number of effective communications processes that can be practised without too much difficulty. These processes can help us overcome the obstacles caused by different perceptions and poor listening – they help us to stay 'on the same wavelength' as the person we are dealing with.

- **Stop talking** – you can't listen while you are talking. It's very easy to get carried away by our own thoughts so try to pause at frequent intervals and give the other person a chance to react. Some people never invite a response from the person they are talking to and then express surprise when people switch off from them. So think about shutting up and asking a few more questions.

- **Give your listener an overview or summary of what you want to say** before launching into detail. This allows the other person the chance to put into context what you are saying.

- **Put yourself in their shoes** – empathize with the other person – when someone is trying to explain something put yourself in their position. Understand and see what they are REALLY trying to communicate. The ability to empathize is critical when dealing with difficult or emotional situations.

- **If you want to speak, use body language to get attention**, e.g. raise the palm of your hand and say "Can I comment on that?" and pause before commenting. This gives the other person the opportunity to pause and switch their attention to you before you speak.

- **Ask more questions** – when you don't understand what is being said or when you need clarification of a point. This clearly indicates that you are listening as well. However, avoid asking questions that either embarrasses people or illustrates their lack of knowledge unless you feel it is absolutely necessary to defend yourself. Tactics such as these often cause hostility or resentment and so lead to a breakdown of communications.

- **Don't stop listening too quickly** – avoid interrupting people – give them time to finish speaking before launching in yourself.

- **Concentrate on what the person is really saying** – not what you think they are saying. We need to actively focus our attention on their words and feelings.

- **Look at the other person** – watch their face, mouth, eyes and body language. Observing someone's body language can help us understand how they feel about what they are saying.

Mirroring or reflecting back their body language in a sensitive manner will help you to show that you are listening and trying to develop a rapport. But don't simply mimic their behaviour as this might provoke a very different response.

- **Summarize what the other person has said at key intervals** – this helps us to clarify our understanding and avoid any potential misunderstandings.

- **Leave any emotional baggage behind** – if we can, we need to try to push our emotions, fears or problems outside the meeting room. Emotional factors often prevent us from listening effectively. But at other times recognize that we may well need to discuss people's feelings in order to get to the real issues.

- **Control your anger** – try not to get angry at what is being said. Whilst anger can be a positive force it can often prevent us from actively listening and developing a full understanding of what is being said. If you do feel strongly about an issue, recognize your feelings but try to isolate them and control them during the discussion.

- **Remove distractions** – put down any papers or pencils you have in your hands as they can cause distractions when communicating. There is a risk we may start pointing!

- **Focus on the critical points** – concentrate on the important ideas and not the detailed points. Of course detail is important, but it is often not as important as the critical points being made in a discussion. Getting agreement or understanding of the big issues is often the breakthrough in discussions. So examine the detail but try to use it to subsequently prove, support or define the main thrust of what is being said or agreed.

- **Don't begin by stating that you disagree** – people will only hear this negative stance and the strategy often provokes an unreceptive response from others. Instead we need to explain our position first and then add why we might find it necessary to disagree with a colleague.

- **Share responsibility for effective communications** – only part of the responsibility for communication lies with the person speaking; as a listener we have an equally important role. Work hard at understanding what is being said and if you don't, ask for clarification.

- **Evaluate the facts and evidence** – as you listen, try to identify not only the significance of the facts and evidence but also their relevance to the discussion.

- **React to ideas, not to people** – don't allow your reactions to the person speaking to influence your interpretation of what they are saying. Remember someone else's ideas or opinions may be valid even if you don't like the person or the way they look.

- **Use the speaking and listening differential** – we can all listen faster than we can talk. By using this differential to our advantage we can really stay focused and concentrate on what has been said. Our speech rate is 100 to 150 words per minute; our ability to listen and think is up to 250 to 500 words per minute.

- **Listen to how something is said** – we frequently concentrate so hard on what is said that we miss the importance of the emotional reactions and attitudes being voiced in someone's speech. In certain cases the attitudes and emotions surrounding a situation may be more important than the words being spoken.

- **Listen for what is not said** – sometimes we can learn just as much by determining what the other person has not said as by what they have said. But in doing this we need to be aware of the dangers of selective interpretation, so we need to listen incredibly hard not just for the facts but also the feelings and if possible the underlying values being expressed.

- **Don't antagonize the other person** – we can cause someone else to conceal their ideas, emotions or attitudes by antagonizing them. This might be achieved by arguing, criticizing or not asking questions. So we have to be aware of the effect we are having on the other person.

- **Listen for the real person** – one of the best ways of finding out about a person is to listen to them talk. By listening to someone talk we can begin to discover what they like and dislike, what their motivations are, what their values are and what makes them tick.

- **Avoid jumping to assumptions** – the old adage states that assumptions can make an ASS out of U and ME. Assumptions can be extremely dangerous so don't assume other people use words the same way you do, 'they didn't say what they meant, but you understand what they meant'. Don't assume that they are avoiding looking you in the eye because they are telling a lie; that they are trying to embarrass you by looking you in the eye; that they are lying because they have interpreted the facts differently than you have, or that they are angry because they are enthusiastic in presenting their views. Assumptions like these may turn out to be true, but more often they just get in the way of clear understanding.

- **Avoid stereotyping the other person** – too often we try to box a person to fit everything they say into what makes sense to us. They are a 'compromiser' or 'difficult person'. Therefore, our perceptions of what they say or mean are all shaded by whether we like or dislike people and their general approaches. At times, it helps in understanding people to know their values and motivations, but we all have the capacity to be unpredictable and to not fit into convenient stereotypes, so beware.

- **Recognize your own prejudices** – try to be aware of your own feelings towards other people and allow for these prejudices.

- **Avoid quick judgments** – wait until you have established all the facts before making any judgments on a person or situation.

- **Identify the influencing style being used** – listen for the influencing style being used by the speaker: logic, emotion, authority, aggression.

Applying classic questioning techniques

The ability to ask questions is perhaps one of the most under-utilized skills in communications. Great managers have the ability to ask brilliant questions and we can all become more effective at asking questions of others. The ability to ask questions allows us to achieve a number of objectives that are all vital in communicating with others:

- Gather information on issues.

- Explore peoples' feelings and attitudes.

- Provoke thought and further discussion.

- Help someone think through a problem.

- Seek clarification on a point or issue.

- See how somebody reacts or responds to our ideas, approach or style.

As already emphasized we are far too inclined to talk rather than ask questions, so developing a toolkit of effective questioning techniques can be a valuable asset. Listed below are the classic types of questions we might use:

- Open-ended: so how do you view the situation? What do you think about the proposal?

- Closed: so you have a problem with the plan then? So you agree with the proposal then?

- Extending: in addition to the cost concerns what other issues worry you?

- Leading: so as you see the strengths of the approach you can agree with the next steps?

- Loaded: so you clearly dislike the design?

- Multiple: so I would like to get your reactions to the timescales and the resourcing issues as well as your overall view of the project?

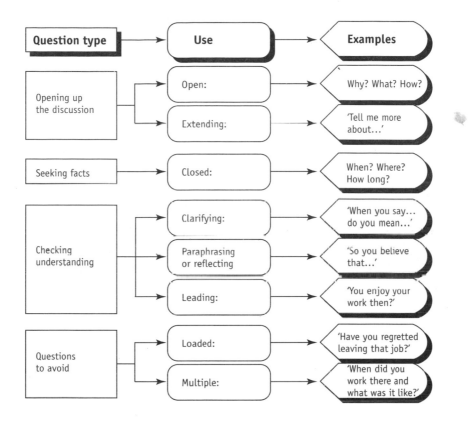

Question type	Use	Examples
Opening up the discussion	Open:	Why? What? How?
	Extending:	'Tell me more about...'
Seeking facts	Closed:	When? Where? How long?
Checking understanding	Clarifying:	'When you say... do you mean...'
	Paraphrasing or reflecting	'So you believe that...'
	Leading:	'You enjoy your work then?'
Questions to avoid	Loaded:	'Have you regretted leaving that job?'
	Multiple:	'When did you work there and what was it like?'

Action point

How to answer questions with confidence

- Thank the person for their question and pause for a moment to reflect and gather your thoughts.

- Repeat the question to confirm that you have understood it correctly.

- Answer the question as best as you can – being direct and clear.

- Check with the person that you have answered the question to their satisfaction – remember this is not the same as providing them with the answer they wanted!

- Thank the individual for their question and interest.

Auditing your listening skills

Below is a quick guide to identifying if you are a good or bad listener. To improve your skills apply the rules and avoid the negative behaviours, or at least be conscious of them.

Key listening rules	The bad listener	The good listener
Try to identify areas of common interest or ground	Rejects boring subjects	Asks 'What's in it for me?'
Assess the content of what is said and not just the delivery	Rejects message and information if the delivery is poor or distracting	Listens for content. Able to overcome errors and mannerisms
Don't evaluate too quickly what is said	Argues	Clarifies before commenting
Listen for any ideas that may lie behind what is being said	Listens only for facts, concepts or feelings	Listens for issues and themes behind the details
Avoid external distractions	Is easily distracted	Fights or avoids distractions, tolerates bad habits and knows how to concentrate

Exercise your brain when faced with something new or difficult	Rejects/refuses difficult materials	Views complex material as a challenge/opportunity to learn
Try to stay open-minded	Rejects emotional words or issues	Interprets emotionally charged words or statements. Does not ignore them

Understanding the impact of non-verbal communications

*You cannot **not** communicate – the way we move and use our physiology sends lots of messages and we need to recognize this fact.*

The non-verbal signs or body language that we give when communicating has a powerful impact on any communications process. In order to understand the non-verbal messages we send we need to consider the following signals:

Eye contact

Typically, when people are talking they do not look at the listener all the time. Rather, they will focus around the individual to gauge reaction, then give a longer look to signal that they expect some verbal response. Eye contact by the listener suggests real interest. A steady gaze is often associated with trust and confidence. However, in some situations a sustained gaze could be interpreted as a stare and possibly even aggressive, if other non-verbal behaviours do not give a more sympathetic impression.

Physical proximity

The notion of physical proximity of course varies in different cultures. So for some people 'keeping your distance' may appear naturally polite, for others, a sign of remoteness and even hostility. The safest guideline is to try to establish a comfortable distance, but bear in mind that if you keep backing away to preserve your 'personal space', your actions may be misinterpreted.

Body posture

The body posture that we adopt can convey a lot of information about how we feel or think about a situation. Crossed arms, for instance, are often viewed as a sign of defensiveness – at the same time they can simply mean that we are comfortable. Conversely, open arms are likely to suggest interest and concern. Leaning forward can demonstrate interest, although when overdone it may be seen as threatening. Leaning back can show either disinterest, or a relaxed posture depending on other cues such as the level of questions being asked.

Leaning forward too much can suggest aggression, whereas leaning forward gently indicates interest in what is being said and can do much to build rapport.

Action point

How you use your physiology – the way you move, speak and project energy is a major component of influencing other people. Skilled influencers often project strong levels of physical energy. When they move they use their body language in a positive manner. They don't slouch or appear slow or laid back.

- They offer a strong and firm handshake.

- They speak with an effective voice tone and vary the pace to emphasize key points.

- They move swiftly and with energy.

- They gesticulate and use strong hand movements – forcefully tapping a table, using firm hand movements to people.

- They using sweeping hand movements to involve people.

- They will invade other people's space – moving in on them to impose themselves.

- They stand up in meetings and walk around.

So think about your body language and physiology and how you project energy to other people. Can you do more to project energy and influence?

Physical gestures

Physical gestures can vary a lot between cultures and are therefore a potential minefield. But there are some classic behaviours we can all look out for. For example, a nodding head is usually taken in most Anglo Saxon cultures as a sign of agreement or understanding. In addition, by nodding you will usually encourage someone else to continue talking. In contrast the classic 'looking at your watch' can signal boredom or a need to move on and, when used, provided the person is sensitive to these things will usually bring proceedings to a swift conclusion.

Also watch for classic symptoms such as:

- Folded arms (disinterest, bored – although in some cultures this denotes attention and respect).

- Leaning back in a chair (relaxed and comfortable).

- Head in hands (boredom, disinterest).

- No eye contact (bored, shy, lacking confidence, distrust – just from this simple list you see the potential dangers of misinterpreting such behaviours).

Hands

When someone's hands are not used in conjunction with their speech this can indicate a nervousness and a need to develop further rapport. Conversely, we will all be familiar with hand wringing or clenched knuckles as indicating anxiety or mounting tension.

The movement of hands to the face or mouth can also indicate some form of discomfort or stress. Possibly touching an ear lobe indicates a negative evaluation with what has been said or a refusal to accept the information. Some people argue that a hand to mouth when they are speaking suggests that a lie or untruth is being spoken.

Stroking the chin is believed to indicate thought and a weighing up of what is being said. Whereas when an index finger is pointed vertically towards a lip and the other fingers rest underneath the chin suggests that a critical evaluation is taking place.

Facial expressions

These are perhaps more obvious than other cues, since we all know how to 'look bored' and show 'delight'. So as well as trying to spot others' behaviours try to remain aware of your own facial expressions and use them to your advantage. The effective deployment of facial expressions can be critical in negotiating or sales type meetings. If you sense problems with another person as a result of their expressions check them out, "You look surprised, shocked by that comment?"

Voice tone and other verbal cues

"That's very interesting" spoken in a monotone voice is unlikely to convince anyone that you are interested in what they are saying. So don't betray any personal feelings or opinions though your voice tone as it is an easy give away to other people.

"Mm", "aha" every now and again will help to keep your speaker talking. Avoid "err" or "ugh" as they can sometimes suggest a lack of confidence, or lack of attention.

CHAPTER FIVE

Mastering role reviews and coaching techniques

Mastering role reviews and coaching techniques

Appraising your people

An overview

Appraising individual performance is perhaps the most critical management activity we can undertake as it can lead to promotion and advancement, salary increases, transfers or, in some cases, dismissal. Underlying all performance management and appraisal systems is the assumption that we all want to know how we are doing in our day-to-day work. However, despite this, performance appraisal processes and interviews in particular do not enjoy universal popularity with managers. Whilst most managers enjoy giving good news to their staff there are many managers who dislike and so avoid having to give any bad news.

In examining performance appraisals we prefer to use the term 'role review' as it reflects the move away from the notion of 'job review'; which tends to have connotations of rigid boundaries and territorial ownership. Roles differ to jobs in the sense that they are more dynamic and suited to the current organizational need for flexibility and responsiveness.

The objectives of role reviews

If any role review is to be of value it must be grounded in the current and future work context and challenges, and must result in the following outcomes:

- The identification of current and future role challenges, priorities and deliverables.

- Agreement on plans for resolving problem issues or priority areas.

- The identification of any learning, development or training needs.
- Planned and agreed actions to meet training and learning needs.

In achieving the above, the interview should ideally focus on the future and draw on past experiences, achievements or failures as a means of clarifying improvement actions. Success in any review depends on the extent to which an atmosphere of openness, trust and mutual respect can be established between a manager and colleague. So it pays to focus on the respective benefits of the process to each party.

THE INDIVIDUAL

We all like to know how we are performing in our work and most people enjoy having an opportunity to discuss their work in detail and to explore how they might improve and develop their abilities and potential.

THE MANAGER

For managers the role review helps us to achieve a full understanding of our colleagues views on their performance and work. We also benefit from the discussion on future aspirations and being able to identify any additional resources or guidance needed to advance performance.

The process helps us as managers to understand any individual areas of confusion or overlap with regard to the overall team. More importantly it provides an opportunity to review individual performance in detail as opposed to the casual five minute 'snapshot' discussions that characterize many day-to-day management activities. When done well the role review is all about quality management time.

THE ORGANIZATION

For the organization, role reviews help generate stronger working relationships and links individual efforts to overall corporate performance. The process also focuses on the corporate priorities as well as identifying people with potential.

Structuring a role review

In any role review it is important to ensure that:

- The meeting provides the right environment for the manager and individual to exchange views in an open and constructive manner.

- A forward planning element is a primary target.

- Past performance plays an important but secondary focus.

- The manager provides coaching and guidance.

Too many managers think that a review can be conducted without much preparation and conducted 'on the run'. This approach invariably fails. Preparation is key to getting the best result from the process. You have to have done some homework, established the facts and identified any performance issues. Too many role reviews fail because managers do not plan properly and fail to set aside adequate time to run the meeting.

It is important to also remember that any role review places the manager under review. Staff will be looking to see if their manager has considered the process an important enough event to invest quality time to prepare. A lack of preparation on a manager's part might be rightly interpreted by staff as showing a lack of interest in them.

A typical structure for a role review meeting

Meeting Phase	Initiative taken by Role Holder / Manager		Principal Activity	Balance of Time Spent on Activity During the Meeting
Past Performance Review	50%	50%	1 Review overall progress in a 3 or 6 month period 2 Review key tasks and achievements 3 Check results against targets 4 Consider performance and future challenges	25-35%
Future Targets and Development Plans	60%	40%	5 Identify current issues, obstacles, challenges to future performance 6 Develop new agreed perform-ance plans and targets from previous results 7 Identify any other issues of concern 8 Identify development and learning needs 9 Personal coaching and guidance provided by manager	65-75%

There may be some reviews where it seems that there are so many problems to be discussed, that even three or four hours would not be long enough. In such extreme cases it is advisable to restrict the meeting to say two hours and make arrangements for another separate meeting.

Action points

THE KEY ELEMENTS OF SUCCESSFUL ROLE REVIEWS

- There needs to be a formal structure to the review meeting.
- The role holder needs to feel at ease, and be encouraged to participate and take the initiative.
- Interruptions should be avoided at all costs.
- The room should be comfortable and reflect the right atmosphere – not next to the production department.
- The discussion needs to have a future orientation rather than be an inquest or post-mortem on the past.
- The meeting needs to be seen as an integral part of the organization's normal process for managing people and performance.

Getting ready for a role review interview

PREPARING FOR THE INTERVIEW

Prior to any review you should have agreed a time with your team member and asked them to think through their role, current performance and work problems, and identify where they think they need help. In your role as a coach you should prepare by reviewing:

- Records of performance.
- Projects they have been involved with.
- Future workloads and problems.
- Possible development opportunities.
- The environment and arrangements for the interview.

At this stage of the process you should refrain from pre-judging the performance even though this will be difficult. Save any thoughts or opinions you may have until you have got the views of your team member at the interview.

Conducting a role review and performance management meeting

A checklist for good practice

PLANNING AND PREPARATION

- Review your colleague's performance well in advance of the meeting.
- Identify some key issues from your managerial perspective.
- Identify the positives as well as the development issues.
- Rehearse any negative feedback – apply negative feedback rules – specific and examples provided.
- Prepare some simple notes to help keep you on track.
- Agree a suitable meeting time – avoid particularly pressurized days.
- Set sufficient time aside – one-two hours.
- Get in the right frame of mind – positive, opportunity to discuss teamwork and development etc.
- Opportunity to give positive feedback.
- Recognize it is an important if not urgent activity that most people enjoy.

THE MEETING – INTRODUCTION

- Shut off calls and action do not disturb instructions etc.
- Get into the right frame of mind – focused, positive and relaxed.
- Be clear as to the issues you would like to explore as the manager.

- Welcome and thank your colleague for their time and the opportunity.

- Confirm and set out the purpose and timing of the meeting.

- Emphasize the focus of the discussion is on development and improving the effectiveness of how we all work together – a desire to improve teamwork etc across the business.

- Highlight any competences that were used in any assessment models of effective behaviours and skills – again stress the business objective of raising our corporate-wide skills and capability.

- Again stress that the session is about development as well as an appraisal process – need to discuss individual and unit business objectives, career planning etc.

- Emphasize the confidentiality of the discussion.

- Stress your desire for openness and a quality discussion.

- Highlight the outcomes of the discussion – agreement on some actions – personal brand plan.

- Check with colleague if they are OK with the objectives and purpose.

THE MEETING – THE FEEDBACK DISCUSSION

- Set out some key principles first – need to maintain a balance on the positive feedback as well as any negatives. Want to promote strengths as well as identify any improvement areas.

- Stress your desire to get colleague's reactions, views and to discuss and explore the various issues with them.

- Begin by asking your colleague for their reaction of their performance.

  What do you think about your contribution and performance?

- Focus the first part of the discussion on the strengths of the person.

  What do you see as your positives and strengths?

- Keep the energy focused on your colleague by using a series of probing comments and questions to get them to give you their interpretation of the feedback:

  - Oh... could you say a little bit more as to why you think that?

  - So that surprised you?

  - Have there been any other surprises?

  - What specifically do you consider your strengths?

  - Why do you think that might be an issue?

  - So you were pleased with that?

  - Do you think you are prone to act in that way at times?

- Avoid diving in or taking the lead in the discussion: keep the energy with your colleague. Listen and remember you do not have to do all the talking.

- Apply the 80-20 principle in the conversation: you should only be talking for 20% of the time.

- Get agreement around the strengths and development issues before moving to discuss possible solutions.

- Offer your views but speak for yourself not others, use "I" – "I do sometimes see you being too detail focused." Avoid, "It has been reported or commented on that..." type comments.

- Build on the themes being voiced by your colleague and develop the discussion – avoid jumping to new topics or issues too quickly – see it as a conversation rather than a heavily driven agenda.

- Ask your colleague to summarize the feedback and discussion. So, "What is this all telling you in terms of your strengths and areas to work on?"

- Add your own managerial team leader's perspective, "I would like you to be more participative in the project planning... Yes I think you could do more of ... and less of ..." but be specific.

- Get agreement to the conclusions before beginning to explore possible action plans and a development plan.

- Consider the Stop, Start and Continue structure and explore lots of options, not just formal training.

- Consider: "On the job experiences, coaching with a colleague, self study, change of responsibilities, new tasks to help develop skills, regular review sessions, secondments etc.

- As the manager, offer suggestions and guidance but don't dictate. Ensure your colleague is committed before agreeing to any actions. They should own any solutions not you.

- Agree the actions and commit them to writing – be specific – to do what, by when, to what standard?

- Confirm review periods to follow up: invite any final comments and thank your colleague for his/her time.

Dealing with reactions during a role review

Insufficient skill on your part, or your team member, may result in difficult reactions during a review. The way in which you deal with such reactions will either destroy the review or put it back on track. Listed below are some typical reactions that you might experience and suggested responses for dealing with them:

- **Your team member accepts your assessment and is willing to improve.** The majority of people will react in this way provided the review discussion has been objective and constructive. Even so, do not underestimate the need to provide positive feedback and praise. At the same time, prepare some new opportunities and challenges to discuss.

- **The team member disagrees with your views and supplies facts to support their case.** In this situation total agreement may be impossible to achieve during the discussion. Areas of agreement should be confirmed and areas of disagreement should be freely discussed. At the end of the session you may need to say, "We'll leave that aside and I'll check on the facts and we can meet again". But if the person is right you may have to simply accept that you got it wrong and agree with them. If you agree to go away and check up on some issues you must ensure that you do follow up. Otherwise you'll lose credibility in the eyes of your colleague.

- **Your team member accepts criticism too easily; adopting a passive role and accepting criticism without responding.** This can be a real problem in that you may feel the individual is not taking the review seriously. To counter this you might ask the individual to summarize your criticisms and to comment on them further. In certain cases you might want to provoke some kind of reaction from them by employing a slightly provocative statement such as, "You don't seem very interested or bothered by all of this" or "What do you think will happen if this situation continues?" This might well generate a reaction.

- **Your team member denies any negative criticisms you are making and passes the buck onto some other colleague.** Buck passing is a common flaw with people who are faced with receiving negative feedback. If you do not feel the individual is justified in arguing such a case, you should analyze together and in depth one or more of the specific circumstances to get to the fundamental problem. At the same time be prepared that in some circumstances your colleague may be fully justified in rejecting the feedback.

- **Your team member reacts emotionally.** If someone gets angry or emotional because of having to hear negative criticism don't argue back with them or disapprove. Simply remain calm and absorb any outburst by quietly listening. If the individual becomes too emotionally upset to continue, stop the interview and resume it at a later date. Alternatively, let the emotions subside naturally during the conversation and carry on with the review.

Remember, in some cases people will break down to avoid confronting difficult news. In effect they may be trying to manipulate you to give up the session by appealing to your emotions. In such situations be careful as invariably you may well have to deal with the issue another day. So if you expect anger or tears be prepared in advance – give the person the chance to compose themselves and continue in a calm manner. If necessary offer them a cup of coffee or water but make sure you continue in a composed and relaxed manner.

- **Your team member is very passive and unresponsive.** This response may require you to remove any fears or misunderstandings that may be present by further explaining what the review is about. If this does not create a positive response you should concentrate on anything in which the individual shows an interest, even if to start with it is not related to the purpose of the review. You need to find out why they are reacting as they are. Are they bored, fed up or annoyed about something?

A quick summary guide to running successful role reviews

HAVE A POSITIVE ATTITUDE

- Be clear that the review is for the benefit of the individual, yourself, and your organization.

- Expect the results of the review to have a positive impact.

- Look at the review as an essential part of your role as a professional manager.

BE PREPARED

- Spend time and effort preparing for each review. Think of the effort you would like your manager to put into the process.

- When analyzing the individual's performance list major strengths and weaknesses, then identify specific examples of each. Provide specific suggestions for future action.

- Use a performance review form as a working tool to document points and agreed actions.

- Arrange a time for the review and provide a copy of the performance review form so your team member can also be prepared and be ready to compare performance notes.

CONDUCT AN OPEN REVIEW

- Be honest, objective and constructive.

- Promote a genuine discussion Allow people to present their ideas and listen to them. Be willing to change your position if your facts are proved wrong.

- Keep comments specific. Relate them to the performance and goals set during the last review session and to the individual's performance. Comments should be consistent with the feedback received during their normal day-to-day work. Springing surprises on unsuspecting people only creates bigger problems!

- Avoid statements based on personality unless they really do impact on job performance. If they do, be descriptive. Describe the effect on job performance, not the personality problem. For example, "The way you speak to customers is too aggressive, for example, last week you said to..." This type of specific feedback is much more constructive than saying you have a bad attitude, as it forces the individual to respond to your specific observations.

- Avoid the tendency to omit negative comments for fear of being disliked. The purpose of the review is to help the individual: by avoiding the unpleasant, you only hurt the individual and yourself. Don't run from the unpleasant elements. If you don't, you will almost invariably have to face them at another time and the chances are that by then there will be bigger problems.

- Remember that we all have weaknesses and strengths. Discuss both with your people.

Reach an agreement:

- Be sure the other person understands and accepts the review. Let them summarize what was discussed and agreed to be sure that there are no misunderstandings.

- Together you should arrive at a consensus of past performance and a realistic action plan for the future. This plan should include ways to capitalize on their strengths and deal with any problem areas or development needs.

- Both of you should contract to confirm in writing your discussion and any agreements.

Don't forget about it:

- Completion of the review itself does not conclude your obligation. Make sure you provide ongoing support and guidance to the person involved.

- Follow up later with the individual to ensure that agreed action plans were accomplished.

CHAPTER SIX

Mastering poor performers

Mastering poor performers

How to deal with poor performers

Sooner or later all managers, regardless of how effective they are, will have to deal with a difficult person or poor performer. Many managers feel deeply uncomfortable about giving negative feedback for fear of provoking a hostile reaction, damaging relationships or simply upsetting someone. But a fact of life is that managing people sooner or later involves telling people things that they may not want to hear: so giving negative feedback in a positive and constructive manner severely tests a manager's people skills. It is crucial, therefore, to know not just how to do it but also how to deal with the problems that can arise. Dealing with poor performers requires us to draw on our knowledge and skills in setting objectives and influencing others.

Classic 'problem people' types that we may have to deal might include the:

- **Excuse giver:** I couldn't because of x or y......
- **Fault finder:** But it was the fault of the logistics department.
- **Whinger:** But the equipment was not up to the right quality.
- **Late deliverer:** It will be ready in another week, I promise.
- **Incompetent:** Sorry I didn't realize it was incorrect.
- **Slow learner:** I just need a bit more time to get the hang of things.

Each of these characters must be dealt with in a structured and formal manner if they are to be made to realize the error of their ways.

Managing poor performers – a quick route map

Establish the performance gap	• Check the facts on actual performance.
	• Check the objectives you previously agreed.
	• Focus on the facts and issues, not the personality.
Explore the performance gap	• Use open-ended questions (what, when, where, how and who).
Ask	• Why is it happening? What factors are generating the performance gap?
Listen to the answers being provided	• Find out whether the problem is due to:
	– personal grievances
	– personal problems (ill health, home difficulties etc)
	– outdated rules/procedures/ processes
	– genuine discipline problem
	– personality(s) clashes
	– unclear objectives
	– need for more training or help on the job
	– incompetence
Eliminate the performance gap	• Agree an improvement plan with timescales and clear objectives

Agreeing performance targets

Having discussed any performance problems the next step for a manager is to agree some clear objectives and new performance targets. Using the classic SMART acronym helps to focus the whole process.

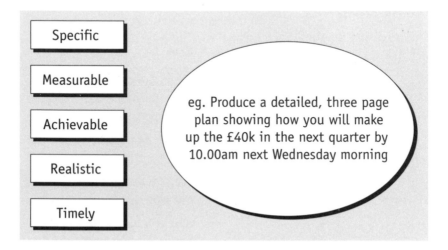

Specific

Measurable

Achievable

Realistic

Timely

eg. Produce a detailed, three page plan showing how you will make up the £40k in the next quarter by 10.00am next Wednesday morning

If it is a grievance or personal problem which is causing the poor perform-ance then try to resolve the problem on the spot by dealing with whatever is worrying the person, or promise to go away and think the issue through. Ensure that you come back to them with a response or answer within an agreed period of time.

Other poor performance caricatures

THE TYPE	THEIR BEHAVIOUR
Roger the Dodger	"Didn't you get my message." Always trying to avoid the issue or problem.
The Injured Bystander	"Surely you are not accusing me." Plays the innocent victim by invoking sympathy.
The Confessor	"Yes, I know it's all my fault..." Always willing to take the blame and sacrifice themselves.

The Buck Passer	"Yes, if only sales had not taken so long..." Tries to offset the blame or responsibility on to someone else.
The Part Time Lawyer	"All of us think..." Endeavours to act as the spokesperson for the team. It is not just me who thinks this but everyone else too.
The Fox	Hardly speaks – except to seek further explanation. Never sure of their motives – possibly a political game player.
The Cry Baby	Uses tears and emotion to weaken management's resolve. Will try to push away problems by emotional means – I can't cope with it all, so leave me alone!
The Resigner	"Well, if that's the way you feel I guess I will have to re-consider my position." A dangerous tactic if over played – can only be done if one is confident that they have a really valued skill or knowledge base.
The Depressive	"I know I'm useless..." Like the Confessors, life is generally very hard and difficult. Everything is bad – can take everyone else down with them as well.
The Counter Attacker	"Are you telling me how to do my job?" Generally an aggressive type who reacts critically to any issues – a hard to deal with type.

With each of these people the solution is to:

- Be firm and fair.

- Stick to the facts and get the discussion focusing on the real issues.

- Get the individual involved to explain their specific behaviours and actions, rather than generalities.

- Pin them down to agree and deliver specific changes within stated timescales.

- Monitor their performance on an on-going basis.

How to give negative feedback successfully

Feedback can of course be based on either clear performance measures and standards or opinions, or some form of the two. When providing feedback we must ensure that what we say is fair and based on some form of evidence or fact. Failure to do this may result in conflicts or disputes arising.

To provide effective feedback a manager must also endeavour to show the following attributes:

EMPATHY

By displaying a real ability to listen a manager can project a degree of understanding and empathy. By avoiding and resisting any immediate reactions or judgments and choosing instead to listen, a manager can create a more credible image if the discussion becomes difficult.

RESPECT

No matter how challenging a performance discussion becomes it is critical that a manager protects the dignity and respect of both parties. By sharing feelings and respecting an individual's right to self respect a manager will always maintain their integrity as a leader.

GENUINENESS

It is important that throughout any review process a manager adopts a positive and constructive tone and remains sincere and genuine. The aim has to be to secure a positive result for both parties without damaging people.

Using the praise sandwich technique: a quick checklist

As we have repeatedly argued, whilst it is easy to praise an individual it is often more difficult to give them bad news or feedback on poor performance. The following rules relate to what is commonly called a 'praise sandwich.' Before using this technique it is important to recognize that as a manager you have to be in the business of developing the long–term capability of your staff. If you are two weeks short of dismissing someone then the approach outlined below will not be appropriate. The 'praise sandwich' approach involves a willingness to engage in successful long–term working relationships which are based on developing someone's true capability and potential. Failure to recognize this philosophy may mean that your attempts to use this technique will be seen as a cynical and manipulative management ploy. So the watchword in employing this approach is genuineness and sincerity. If you don't mean it then don't say it!

- **Start with a positive comment on performance** – if positive feedback is registered first with a colleague, any subsequent negative comment is more likely to be listened to and acted upon.

- **Then provide any negative feedback that you may need to give but be specific and focus only on the individual's behaviour.** Pinpoint behaviour that people are able to actually action and change, e.g. "In chairing meetings you tend to talk over people." Follow this feedback with specific examples:

  "In last Monday's finance meeting, for example, several times John tried to comment on the budget allocation and you interrupted him and failed to let him make his point. Also in last week's sales presentation, three times the customer wanted to ask a question and you failed to recognize their need."

- **Describe the event as clearly as possible and avoid emotion and judgmental language**, e.g. "You gave unclear instructions with regard to the next steps in the project as illustrated by the confusion over the timetable that subsequently followed." Don't evaluate the behaviour by using emotive language such as, "You gave terrible or useless instructions." This always has the potential to inflame feelings and provoke a more hostile response.

- **Use 'I' statements** – "I feel that you..." or "I am annoyed by the fact that you went against a previous agreement." The use of 'I' in feedback gives it more impact and so is more likely to be listened to – after all it is your view that you are expressing so own it!

- **Ask whether the other person can see your point of view** and where you are coming from.

- **Suggest alternative ways that your colleague might approach the issue or problem in the future.** Provide some clues about the outcome you would prefer so as to coach them towards a solution. If the ideas or solutions are not forthcoming then you may need to be directive and point out the required improvement standards that you are seeking.

- **Don't overload your colleague** – people can only handle up to three pieces of negative feedback in one session. So keep it sharp and focused.

- **Lastly, close the sandwich by offering a final positive comment** – but again use this approach with genuineness and sincerity, e.g. "Anyway let's look forward to the project presentation as I am getting lots of positive comments on what you have been doing with regard to the design phase."

- **Recognize that the final positive comment might not be appropriate** if you believe that the negative feedback you have given warrants the individual to really reflect on their behaviour and subsequent response. So think about the kind of impact you are seeking to create. But recognize that for many simple day-to-day activities the feedback sandwich can be a useful tool if used appropriately.

Receiving feedback

Just as giving feedback to others is critical so is our ability to receive it. When we receive feedback we have the capacity to be really quite selective in what we want to hear. To avoid this problem we can observe the following rules:

- First listen to the message and postpone any initial knee-jerk reactions.

- Be clear about what's being said to you. "So if I have understood you correctly you are saying that the report is not technically correct? Have I understood you?"

- Probe until there is something you can act on. "Can you provide me with some examples?" "What do you mean when you say people are not happy?"

- Check out with others to verify the validity of the comments or feedback being provided.

- Finally, remember it is your choice whether to accept or reject the feedback. As a manager we cannot force someone to accept our feedback but we can make them aware of any consequences that might follow as a result of failing to heed our advice.

The ten golden rules of feedback

1. FOCUS YOUR FEEDBACK ON THE BEHAVIOUR NOT THE PERSON

When giving feedback always comment on what a person actually does (their behaviours) rather than what we imagine their motives or aims might be.

Focusing on behaviour implies that we use adverbs (that relate to actions) rather than adjectives (that relate to qualities) when referring to an individual. Thus we might say a person "talked a lot in the meeting" rather than this person "is an arrogant loud-mouth".

When we talk in terms of 'personality traits', it implies inherited qualities that are difficult, if not impossible to change. Focusing on behaviours implies something related to a specific situation that could have been changed. It is generally less threatening to hear comments about our behaviour than our 'personality traits'.

2. FOCUS YOUR FEEDBACK ON OBSERVATIONS RATHER THAN 'INFERENCES'

Observations refer to what we visibly see or hear in the behaviour of another person. Inferences are interpretations and conclusions that we make from what we see or hear. Inferences are conclusions about someone that in turn can influence our observations and the feedback we give.

When inferences or conclusions are shared, and it may be valuable to do this, it is important that they are identified as such. We all have filters that we need to be conscious of. For example, John arrived late – he knew the meeting was set for 10:00 – he arrived late deliberately – that is the problem with John, he is not reliable!

So again stick to describing the behaviour and avoid leaps of logic in terms of intended motives.

3. FOCUS YOUR FEEDBACK ON DESCRIPTIONS RATHER THAN JUDGMENTS

Describing a situation means reporting what actually happened. A judgment is often an evaluation of a situation in terms of good or bad or right or wrong. The meeting was a total disaster!! Such judgments arise out of our own personal mental models or values. A description represents neutral (as far as possible) reporting, e.g. "The client did not agree with our proposal and pricing."

4. FOCUS YOUR FEEDBACK ON BEHAVIOUR IN TERMS OF 'MORE OR LESS'

Using a 'more or less' terminology implies a continuum on which any level of behaviour may fall. It is also stressing the issue of quantity, which is objective and measurable. For example, "You could have asked more questions in the meeting." Observations are often more subjective and judgmental.

For example, the participation of a person in a meeting may fall on a continuum of low to high participation, rather than 'good' or 'lousy'. In a business presentation the manager could have asked 'more questions' or 'learnt to shut up'.

5. FOCUS YOUR FEEDBACK IN THE 'HERE AND NOW' TIME DIMENSION

What we do is always tied to a time and place. Feedback is generally more meaningful if given as soon as possible after our observations or reactions take place. This keeps the feedback concrete and relatively free of any distortions that come with the lapse of time. So try to keep your feedback in the 'here and now.

6. IN CERTAIN SITUATIONS FOCUS YOUR FEEDBACK ON SHARING IDEAS AND INFORMATION RATHER THAN SIMPLY GIVING ADVICE

By sharing feedback and information we leave the other party free to decide for themselves how to use the feedback and information. When we give advice as managers we tell people what to do and so take away their freedom to determine what is the most appropriate course of action. In coaching situations it is critical to explore and encourage the other person to come up with their own solutions to problems. As managers sometimes we need to step back from our simple 'advice giving mode'.

7. FOCUS YOUR FEEDBACK ON THE VALUE IT GIVES THE RECIPIENT, NOT THE FEELING OF RELEASE IT MAY PROVIDE YOU WITH!

Any feedback provided should serve the needs of the receiver rather than the needs of the giver. Feedback often needs to be given and heard as an offer, not an imposition. Avoid giving feedback just to make you feel good. Yet recognize there will be times where 'release' is appropriate in order to stress urgency.

8. AVOID FEEDBACK OVERLOAD

To overload a person with feedback is to reduce the possibility that they may use the information given. It may even result in even less confidence and in turn further falls in performance

9. GIVE FEEDBACK AT THE RIGHT TIME

The use of personal feedback involves emotional reactions so it is always important to be aware of the timing of feedback. Excellent feedback presented at an inappropriate time will always lose its impact. So choose carefully – the bigger the message the more sensitive the timing.

10. FOCUS YOUR FEEDBACK ON 'WHAT IS SAID' RATHER THAN 'WHY IT IS SAID'

Feedback that relates to the what, how, when, where, or what of an incident are characteristics we can observe. A focus on 'why' something is said, often takes us from the observable to the inferred world. This then brings up questions of 'motive' or 'intent'. For example, "Why are you saying this to me?"

To make assumptions about the motives of people giving us feedback may prevent us from hearing the feedback. Equally it may cause us to distort what is said. If I question 'why' a person is giving me feedback, I may not hear what they are actually saying.

CHAPTER SEVEN

Mastering team management

Mastering team management

An introduction to team performance

In the rapidly changing world of business where organization structures and processes are in a state of constant change there is an ever increasing emphasis on team work. Today's organization necessitates the constant creation and break up of temporary teams. Whilst teams have always been important, the focus now placed on project work and matrix structures means that team work assumes far greater significance. Managers are expected to establish and develop teams more rapidly than ever. They are under pressure to motivate their teams and to drive them to higher levels of performance. This team focus looks set to continue and so managers need to become a lot smarter at understanding the characteristics and dynamics of high performance teams.

So let's begin by defining a team. A team may be defined as a unified group of people with a common goal or purpose and identity. In turn each team member is committed to working together and has their own areas of responsibility and accountability. In effect they need each other in order to succeed. In some respects we can compare a work team with a football team. To score goals and win the game a team has to play together. This means passing the ball to one another in order to move the team forward and eventually score. It also means that individuals have to chase back and support others when possession is lost to the other team. Selfish and overly individualistic behaviour will not guarantee success. In football terms it is not just the team with the most talent that so often wins. Rather it is the team who practises well, plays for each other and supports the overall team effort who often win. Just as a football team practises and reviews past performances, so a work team should also review its performance and learn from mistakes. Any manager in today's fast moving business world needs to be able to form teams quickly and in so doing create an atmosphere of strong and productive working relationships. In helping a team to function effectively the leader needs to provide the following:

- Clear objectives and roles for the team and individual members.

- An informal but effective working atmosphere.

- Time-lines and control processes for guiding the team.

- Regular assessments of both team and individual performance.

- Rewards for performance – both for the team as a whole and individuals.

- Development and coaching to continually raise performance standards.

Good managers will spend large amounts of time managing their teams but, regardless of the investment, sooner or later they will encounter problems in the way the team works. All teams have their good and bad periods and it is the sign of a good manager who can lead a team through a difficult patch and bring their performance back up to standard. When a team does becomes derailed in terms of performance we might hear the following comments being voiced either by the manager or team members:

- "They just don't seem to be working for each other."

- "The team meeting is just another opportunity for people to moan about their needs."

- "Our best ideas seem to get totally lost in the meetings."

- "They just don't seem interested or motivated in what we have to do."

- "There are too many hidden agendas!"

- "People are not being honest and upfront with each other!"

- "Absolutely chaotic!! We do not seem to have an agreed sense of direction or purpose."

- "Some people are not getting on with each other and it is impacting on the overall team."

Whilst all teams experience some of these issues at one time or another the prolonged presence of such problems might indicate more underlying problems. An effective manager would need to be able to get on top of these problems at an early stage so as not to drag the team down in a negative spiral. To help stay alert to such problems it can help to understand some of the classic elements of team development and processes. Awareness of such issues can mean a manager can intervene with a greater sense of purpose if problems start to develop.

Team development

A classic approach to team development and processes was originally formulated by Bruce Tuckman in the 1960s and updated in the 1970s. Whilst the model has been around for a long time it is widely regarded as a definitive approach to helping us understand the different stages that teams go through in their development. By understanding this development process, managers can adopt different strategies to help guide their teams through the various stages.

Tuckman's model is based on four sequential stages of development that all teams experience:

1. Forming stage

2. Storming stage

3. Norming stage

4. Performing stage

THE CLASSIC TEAM DEVELOPMENT CYCLE

FORMING	STORMING	NORMING	PERFORMING
• Impersonal	• Losing team members	• Developing skills	• Tolerance
• Guarded	• Difficulties	• Getting organized	• Open
• Polite	• Opting out	• Systems established	• Flexible
• Watchful	• Confronting	• Task focus	• Maturity
	• Managing conflicts	• Confronting issues	• Sharing
	• Feeling stuck	• Agreed procedures	• Energy

Testing ⟶ Infighting ⟶ Sharing and Doing ➤ Performing

Source: BW Tuckman

Tuckman's model advocates a range of specific actions to support each development phase. By adopting these strategies a manager can optimize the team's performance. The critical point comes in recognizing the development stage the team is in. Listed below are the classic characteristics and leadership team actions associated with each of the four stages.

The forming stage

(Newness, honeymoon, impersonal)

Behavioural characteristics:

- Politeness.

- Superficiality, reserved.

- Avoiding controversy.

- Suspense – what's going to happen to me?

- Withholding of information.

- Watchful of other members – guarded position.

- Relatively low levels of involvement and participation.

- Fear, anxiety, nervousness.

The team leadership issues:

- Dependence on the leader to get things moving.
- Providing direction: moving the team from the comfort of non-threatening topics to encountering the risk of disagreement and potential conflict.

Team and people issues:

- Inclusion – will I be included?
- Who are these people?
- What will happen to me?
- Am I going to enjoy this experience?

Strategies to help a team move through this phase:

- Establish a clear sense of direction and performance goals.
- Identify the resources available to the team.
- Effect introductions – 'break the ice' and get people co-operating.
- Build a supportive and open atmosphere.
- Identify relevant parties and stakeholders outside the team.
- Clarify individual roles, expectations and objectives.
- Get the team doing things together.

The storming stage

(CHALLENGE, CONFLICT, COMPETITION, DIFFICULTIES)
Behavioural characteristics:

- Feeling stuck: "What are we supposed to be doing here?"
- "I'm fed up with this" feelings being expressed.
- Opting out of proceedings.
- Resistance to requests for help and co-operation.

- Competitive behaviour between team members.

- Sub-groups developing.

- Jockeying for position – who's in charge here?

- Differences being expressed openly.

The team leadership issues:

- Feelings of loss of control.

- People opt out or drop out.

- Loss of momentum and impetus.

- Challenging the leader.

- Resistance to move things on.

Team and people issues:

- Allowing the team the opportunity to vent negative feelings.

- Search or battle for control and influence.

- Leadership of the team – avoiding too long a vacuum.

- Sense of frustration and loss of direction.

Strategies to help a team move through this phase:

- Allow the dispute to continue for a while – the team need to vent – it is OK!

- Re-establish and confirm the team's mission and objectives – why we are here.

- Clarify the leadership role.

- Clarify roles, responsibilities and expectations.

- Promote real listening amongst the team.

- Establish required team procedures and processes

- Provide positive feedback.

- Manage the conflict constructively – identify the issues.

- Stay relaxed and calm – see this stage as natural and positive.

- Move the team from 'testing and proving' to a 'problem solving mentality'.

The norming stage

(MATURING, SHARING, GETTING DOWN TO BUSINESS)

Behavioural characteristics:

- Give and take amongst team members.

- Acceptance and agreement on roles and responsibilities.

- Procedures and processes understood by all.

- Ground rules for meetings are set and adhered to.

- Working together.

- Group decision-making is generated by quality discussions.

- Increased levels of active listening occur.

The team leadership issues:

- Inter-dependence between members and the leader.

- Sharing and completing work together.

- Shaping the team as an effective unit.

Team and people issues:

- Support and acceptance of others.

- Sharing perspectives, feelings and ideas.

- Soliciting and giving feedback to each other.

- Creativity and innovation increasing.

- Openness.

- Positive feelings about being part of the team.

- Mutual support.

Strategies to help a team move through this phase:

- Demonstrate 'give and take' amongst team members.

- Discuss team processes and dynamics.

- Ask for input versus 'telling'.

- Focus on team goals and objectives when conflicts arise.

- Demonstrate openness to feedback.

- Re-establish roles and responsibilities.

- Confront issues.

The performing stage

(UNITY, CONFIDENCE, MATURITY, HIGH ENERGY)

Behavioural characteristics:

- High performance and productivity through problem solving strategies.

- Strong mutual support and co-operation.

- Giving and receiving feedback.

- Lots of emotional and task support evident in team working.

- Follow through with regard to commitments and action plans.

- Strong team identity, spirit, pride and cohesion.

- All team members contribute.

- Flexibility in outlook and approach.

- Compliance of the norming stage is replaced by commitment.

The team leadership issues:

- Inter-dependence of the team and leader.

- Role of the leader – redundancy?!

- Need to stand back – delegate and empower.

Team and people issues:

- Commitment.
- Risk taking.
- Trust and support.

Strategies to help a team move through this phase:

- Delegate, coach and develop team members.
- Enhance openness.
- Promote supportive and creative confrontation of ideas.
- Seek out feedback.
- Let go!

How to start up a team building process

To start up a team building session we need to focus on four key steps.

1 ESTABLISH THE PURPOSE AND OBJECTIVES OF THE TEAM – GET PEOPLE WORKING TOGETHER

Team members can often have different levels of commitment and to avoid later conflicts it is a good idea to:

- Detail the fundamental purpose (Mission) and goals (Objectives) for the team.
- Invite each team member to contribute their thoughts about the goals or task.
- Invite the team members to explain their current priorities and assignments.
- Ask team members to commit to the team's priorities. It is better to resolve potential conflicts about availability and commitment sooner rather than later.

- Invite the team to determine a realistic timetable for completing the work.

2 SHARE ANY CONCERNS AND EXPECTATIONS

Invite discussions around any team members concerns. Make any issues part of your team building agenda as this will help ensure a positive and productive working climate. It is important to get any difficult issues out the way at an early stage. Allow team members time to prepare responses to the following questions:

- Do you have any concerns about working on this project with this team?

- How would you like this team functioning if it was working at maximum capability?

- Do you see any potential barriers we face in trying to develop a high performance team?

- What specific actions do we need to take to ensure that we do operate as a highly effective team?

3 CLARIFY THE GOALS

Team goals need to be set to provide direction and unify the team's future efforts. In discussing the goals all members will need to:

- Agree on the central mission and goals of the team.

- Evaluate and commit to all proposed plans and strategies to achieve the goals.

- Discuss and agree the necessary resources and timescales for achieving the team's objectives.

4 DEVELOP OPERATING GUIDELINES

The team also needs to establish a clear set of operating principles and guidelines for operating. The team will need to decide:

- Any operating guidelines for how they will work together.

- Decision making processes that will be used – by team consensus, the team leader or the individual responsible for the task?

- How the work will be assessed and reviewed.

- How individual concerns will be dealt with.

- How potential differences will be resolved – majority vote or leader decision?

- How any revisions to plans will take place.

Once your team building session has been completed and you have agreed a set of operating guidelines your team will be ready to begin working on the overall goals and objectives.

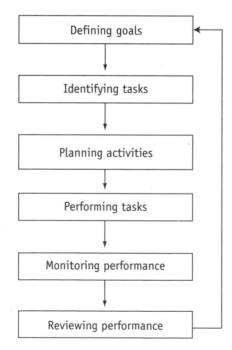

A strategy for day-to-day teamworking

Listed below is a model for operating effective teamwork on a day-to-day basis. Use it as a checklist against which your team can plan, implement and evaluate its activities:

```
        ┌──────────────────────────┐
     ┌─▶│      Defining goals       │◀─┐
     │  └──────────────────────────┘  │
     │              │                  │
     │              ▼                  │
     │  ┌──────────────────────────┐  │
     │  │     Identifying tasks     │  │
     │  └──────────────────────────┘  │
     │              │                  │
     │              ▼                  │
     │  ┌──────────────────────────┐  │
     │  │    Planning activities    │  │
     │  └──────────────────────────┘  │
     │              │                  │
     │              ▼                  │
     │  ┌──────────────────────────┐  │
     │  │     Performing tasks      │  │
     │  └──────────────────────────┘  │
     │              │                  │
     │              ▼                  │
     │  ┌──────────────────────────┐  │
     │  │  Monitoring performance   │  │
     │  └──────────────────────────┘  │
     │              │                  │
     │              ▼                  │
     │  ┌──────────────────────────┐  │
     │  │   Reviewing performance   │──┘
     └──└──────────────────────────┘
```

Defining goals

Whatever the task facing your team, it is essential that you establish clearly defined goals. Of course when setting any goals you must be realistic about the timescales involved and your team's ability and capacity to achieve them.

A TYPICAL ERROR IN GOAL SETTING

A sales team sets demanding sales goals for a trading period. In time these goals prove to be overly ambitious and unrealistic. The result is that the team subsequently fails to hit the targets. This in turn disrupts financial plans and subsequently production schedules. Initially the team responds by increasing activity and exerting more effort. Repeated failure to attain the goals however, results in a loss of morale and in some cases a team or leadership crisis in addition to the significant loss of revenue.

Whilst most teams and their leaders can become overly ambitious when setting objectives, other teams might set goals that are too low. In such instances, as the team goals are always exceeded they result in a lack of challenge or drive for the team's performance.

The lesson is that when setting objectives there is a fine balance between setting unrealistic and achievable goals. All performance goals have to be stretching but also realistic if they are to generate a desirable improvement in individual and team performance.

Identifying tasks

Having defined and agreed our team's goals we need to define the key tasks necessary to deliver the goals. These tasks will either be a series of inter-related and sequential activities or a collection of tasks that need to be performed concurrently.

Planning activities

Planning involves allocating people, time and resources to each key task and the manager or team leader will need to address the following questions:

- What is the most effective and efficient way of organizing ourselves to achieve the team's goals and objectives?

- What is our proposed time-line for completing the various tasks?

- By what process will we track the team's progress against the various tasks that need to be completed?

- What forms of contingency planning do we need to put into place in the event that we fail to deliver in the allotted time schedules we have set?

A typical error in planning is that the team becomes too absorbed in the planning activity itself and so forgets about the need for actual implementation. You cannot plan forever and sooner or later you have to take action to deliver results. So the leader has to ensure that a careful balance is struck between the planning and implementation phases of the work.

Executing new and additional tasks

In any project there is almost an invariable need to perform new and additional tasks that will not have been anticipated in the original planning phase. Projects seldom occur within a vacuum and new developments may often mean that the team has to take on new tasks and workloads. At this stage it will be necessary to re-plan since any new or additional tasks will require additional resources and a juggling of project priorities.

Reviewing performance

At the end of the project we need to review the team's performance, not just in terms of the tasks, but more importantly in terms of our goals and outputs. Have we delivered on what we said we would? The key questions to ask in any review process are:

- Did we achieve our goals?

- If so, how well did we do?

- What could we do differently next time?

- If we failed to achieve our goals, why?

- Were there other factors that prevented us from delivering?

- Did we spend sufficient time planning?

- Were the right tasks identified in our planning phase?

- Did we adequately project manage the plan?

- Were the tasks performed to the correct level?

- Were the goals set realistic?

- How well did the team work together?

Reviewing these questions helps us to learn and to revise our approach and processes for the next challenge or project. To improve team performance it is just as important to identify any reasons for failure, as well as it is to identify the reasons for success. A characteristic of high performance teams is that they do take time out to review their working methods and processes as well as the actual results they achieve, whether they succeed or not. Too often in organizational life we run quickly onto the next problem or challenge without adequately spending time to review and learn from our most recent experiences.

Team working – processes

When we talk of team processes we are talking about the 'How' of working together as a team. Process looks at relationships and communications within a team. Process explores how feelings and disagreements were dealt with within a team. As with running on to the next challenge or project most teams take little time to explore how well their process worked. Below is a checklist of typical process issues that face a team and their leader; it can be used as a means to monitor team performance. A sample list of process characteristics that result from high performance teams is also provided as a reference.

TEAM EFFECTIVENESS – HOW DOES YOUR TEAM RATE?

	Fully Effective				Ineffective
	5	4	3	2	1
• Informal atmosphere					
• Full participation in discussion					
• Task understood and accepted by all					
• Members listen to each other					
• Team resolves disagreements					
• Consensus decision making					
• Frequent and frank criticism					
• Expression of feelings					
• Action planned and commitment given					
• Leadership shifts – manager does not dominate					
• Team is self conscious about its operation					

Crucial process issues facing any team leader

Issues

Questions

The working atmosphere and relationships

What kind of team relationships are required for success? How close, friendly, formal or informal should they be?

Participation levels	How much participation is required of the team? Some people need to do more than others? All have to give equally? Are some members needed more than others? Do we really need to be a team?
Team objectives and commitment	How much do the team members need to understand the goals? How much do they need to accept or be committed to the goals?
Communication and information flows	How is the team to share information? Who needs to know what? Who should listen most to whom?
Conflict management	How should disagreements or conflicts be handled? To what extent should they be resolved?
Decision making	How should decisions be made? Consensus? Processes Voting? One-person rule?
Performance evaluation	How is the team's evaluation to be managed? Everyone appraises everyone else? The leader has total control of the process? A few individuals take responsibility?
Role and task assignments	How are role and task assignments to be allocated? Voluntarily? By team discussion? By the team leader?
Team leadership	Who should lead the team? How should the leadership functions be exercised? Shared? Elected? Appointed from outside?
Process management	How should the team monitor and improve its process management? Ongoing feedback from members? Formal procedures? Regular weekly meetings?

Recognizing why teams fail

The manager's fault

Manager does not:

- Have a clear and compelling vision.
- Set a clear direction with priorities.
- Hold people accountable for their performance.
- Display appropriate supporting behaviours to team members.
- Allocate resources effectively.
- Build the right team atmosphere.
- Hold effective team meetings.
- Share information with people when they need it.
- Deal with negative individual behaviours that conflicts with the team's goals and objectives.
- Understand people's feelings.
- Understand what is really going on in the team.
- Develop people and their potential.
- Manage the interface between the team and the rest of the organization.
- Like getting feedback from team members.

The team's fault

Team members do not:

- Take responsibility for their contributions.
- Recognize their inter-dependence in reaching their goals (they are competitive as opposed to collaborative in their behaviour).

- Possess basic interpersonal skills.

- Confront conflicts and prefer to choose scapegoats outside of the team to blame.

- Develop the technical competence for their position.

- Take responsibility for their part in follow-on action plans.

- Deal with the real issues in the team.

- Put team goals above self-interest.

- Understand the business they are in.

- Participate fully in the team process.

Understanding your team roles

Belbin's team preferences

Through his extensive and world renowned research Professor Meredith Belbin has devised a world recognized method of identifying team preferences which help us to understand why people behave in certain ways in teams. He identified eight types of preference for working in teams. Below are listed some of the essential characteristics of each type:

- The company worker/implementor

- The chair/co-ordinator

- The shaper

- The plant

- The resource investigator

- The monitor evaluator

- The team worker

- The completer finisher

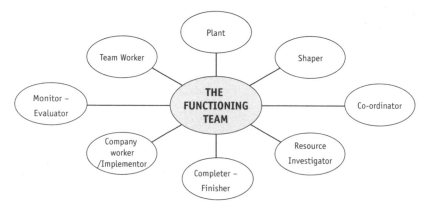

1. The company worker/implementor

Role

- Translates general ideas and plans into practical working objectives.

- Gets down to implementation.

- Breaks things into tasks and actions.

- Delivers actions and results.

Methods

- Helps ensure that the team's objectives have been properly established and that any tasks have been clearly defined.

- Clarifies any practical details and deals with them.

- Maintains a steady, systematic approach to the job at hand.

- Is calm under pressure and reliable – will not let you down.

- Perseveres in the face of difficult and challenging targets. Is tenacious.

- Provides practical support to other team members.

Behaviours to avoid

- Unconstructive criticism of other team members' ideas and suggestions.

- Lack of flexibility. Company workers have a high efficiency concern which means they question the introduction of the 'new'.

- Being resistant to new ideas or innovations.

As a manager, a company worker or implementor's strengths are their ability to define objectives and practical details. They are also very effective in introducing and maintaining procedures and structures. In organizations they are often promoted because of their inherent organizing abilities and skills. They value what organizations like.

2. The chair/co-ordinator

Role

- Controls and organizes the activities of the team, making best use of the resources available.

- Pulls the team together.

- Stands back and helicopters above the team.

- Is able to get people working together.

Methods

- Encourages team members to achieve the team's objectives by helping them identify their roles and contributions.

- Encourages people to put the team's objectives before their own.

- Provides positive feedback on individual performance.

- Smoothes over disagreements and inter-team competition with keen people insight and understanding. Uses tact and diplomacy to control and manage.

- Identifies weaknesses in the team's composition and organizes and develops the team to neutralize any weaknesses.

- Co-ordinates resources.

- Exercises self-discipline and perseverance. Acts as a focal point for the team's effort, especially when under pressure.

- Delegates effectively.

Behaviours to avoid

- Not recognizing the full capabilities of the team. Not using all of the team's resources.

- Competing with other team types.

- Failing to add a creative, innovative or challenging aspect to their role.

- Abdicating the leadership role in the face of strong competition (particularly from shapers and possibly plants).

As a manager, a chair or co-ordinator is in a good position to lead the team. They are comfortable standing back from the detail and can mobilize people to tackle the issues. Their effective interpersonal skills also mean that people will listen and take their lead from an effective chair.

3. The shaper

Role

- Makes things happen.

- Gives shape and strong direction to the team's activities.

- Injects energy and drive into a team's proceedings.

Methods

- Directs the team's focus, setting objectives and clear priorities.

- Adopts a wide perspective of the team's goals and helps individuals understand their roles and contributions.

- Exerts a strong directive influence on the team's discussions.

- Summarizes outcomes in terms of objectives and targets.

- Will often appear impatient and in a rush.

- Focuses on progress and achievements. Intervenes when the team wanders from their objectives.

- Challenges others if they are pursuing another direction.

- Can be argumentative and dismissive of people who do not move as fast.

Behaviours to avoid

- An overly directive style that assumes undue authority.

- Being too directive in making summaries, appraisals or interventions.

- Not being tactful. Avoid being overly blunt or even rude and insensitive to the needs of others.

- Becoming isolated or remote from the team. Losing identity as a team member. Being seen as too egotistic.

- Competing with other team members, particularly the plant and the monitor evaluator.

A shaper performs best when operating in a team of peers. If they find themselves in a formal leadership position they may well need to adopt more Co-ordinator type behaviours. This may require more involvement in routine activities and more self-discipline. Shapers normally focus on a broad brush approach to getting things done. They have little time for the detail and want to drive forward. They also need to watch that their insensitivity to the needs of others does not, in the long-term, create problems for them. Tact and diplomacy is not always a high priority for shapers.

4. The plant

Role

- Acts as a primary source of ideas and innovation for the team.
- Creative – an 'agent provocateur'.
- An independent perspective.

Methods

- Concentrates their attention on the big issues and major strategies.
- Formulates new and often radical ideas and approaches.
- Looks for possible breakthroughs in approaches and methods.
- Times their contributions; presenting proposals at appropriate moments.

Behaviours to avoid

- Attempting to demonstrate their capabilities over too wide a field.
- Contributing ideas for reasons of self-interest and indulgence rather than the team's needs, and so may alienate the team.
- Taking offence when their ideas are evaluated, criticized and possibly rejected. Sulking and refusing to make any further contributions to the team.
- Becoming too inhibited about putting ideas forward, especially in dominant, extrovert, or over-critical groups. Being intimidated or alternatively arguing with Shapers.

A plant needs to exercise self-discipline and be prepared to listen to team members' comments on their ideas and proposals (particularly their Monitor Evaluator colleague(s)). If found in a leadership role a Plant must not let the stresses of controlling the team stifle their creative input.

In non-directive roles a plant should expect to be used as a strong team resource; devoting their energies and talents towards establishing their role as a creative thinker and ideas person.

5. The resource investigator

Role

- Explores the team's outside resources and develops useful contacts for the team.

- Harnesses resources for the team.

- A networker and free agent.

Methods

- Makes excellent contacts quickly. Develops effective and useful relationships and allies for the team.

- Uses their interest in new ideas and approaches to explore outside possibilities. Introduces new people and resources to the team.

- Develops their role as the team's main point of contact with outside groups. Keeps up-to-date with new and related developments that may be helpful to the team's work.

- Helps maintain good relationships in the team and encourages team members to make best use of their talents, especially when the team is under pressure.

Behaviours to avoid

- Becoming too involved with their own ideas at the expense of exploring others.

- Rejecting ideas or information before submitting them to the team.

- Relaxing too much when the pressure is off.

- Getting involved in wasteful or unproductive activities. This often results from the resource investigator's natural sociability.

Resource Investigators are skilled communicators with a creative outlook. They are vital to helping bring new resources into a team and their networking capabilities make them invaluable.

6. The monitor evaluator

Role

- Analyzes ideas and suggestions.

- Evaluates ideas and approaches for their feasibility and practical value.

- Deals with facts.

- Introduces a high level of critical thinking ability to any team.

Methods

- Uses high levels of critical thinking ability to assess issues and plans.

- Balances an experimenting outlook with a critical assessment.

- Builds on others' suggestions or ideas. Helps the team to turn ideas into practical applications.

- Makes firm but practical and realistic arguments against the adoption of unsound approaches to problems.

- Is diplomatic when challenging suggestions.

Behaviours to avoid

- Using their critical thinking ability at the team's expense.

- Tactless and destructive criticism of colleagues' suggestions. Liable to upset others because of this.

- Negative thinking; allowing critical thinking skills to outweigh their openness to new ideas. Provoking a "You always see reasons why it cannot be done!" type of response.

- Competitive behaviour with others.

- Lowering the team's morale by being excessively critical and objective.

A successful monitor evaluator combines high critical thinking skills with a practical outlook. When a monitor evaluator is a team leader they need to ensure that they do not dominate other members of the team and stifle contributions. When in a non-directive role a monitor evaluator has the challenge of making their voice heard and not appearing threatening to colleagues. If they can avoid a tendency towards undue scepticism and cynicism their strengths will help them develop their management capability.

7. The team worker

Role

- Strong team player.

- Helps individual team members to contribute.

- Promotes and maintains team spirit and effectiveness.

Methods

- Applies themselves to the task.

- Observes the strengths and weaknesses of team members.

- Supports team members in developing their strengths, e.g. builds on suggestions and contributions.

- Helps individuals manage their weaknesses with personal advice and assistance.

- Selfless in outlook.

- Improves team communications and builds relationships.

- Fosters a strong sense of team spirit by setting an example.

Behaviours to avoid

- Competing for status or control in the team.

- Aligning with one team member against another.

- Not addressing or resolving conflict situations.

- Delaying tough decisions.

The team worker role can be exercised at different levels within a team. As a manager the team worker should see their role as a delegator and developer of people. Team worker's qualities of conscientiousness and perseverance will help ensure that projects are completed on time, and to the necessary levels of cost and quality. But they have to watch that their sense of duty in wanting to help team members achieve objectives often overrides their concerns for overall task or goal achievements.

8. The completer finisher

Role

- Ensures all the team's efforts are as near perfect as possible.

- Ensures that tasks are completed and that nothing is overlooked.

- Injects urgency into problems and projects that fall behind.

- Provides attention to detail.

Methods

- Perfectionist – looks for errors or omissions; especially those that may result from unclear responsibilities.

- Works on tasks where attention to detail and precision are important.

- Looks for mistakes in detail.

- Actively identifies work or tasks that require more detailed attention.

- Raises the standards of all the team's activities.

- Maintains a sense of urgency and priority.

Behaviours to avoid

- Unnecessary emphasis on detail at the expense of the overall plan and direction.

- Negative thinking or destructive criticism.

- Lowering team morale by excessive worrying.

- Appearing slow moving or lacking in enthusiasm.

A completer finisher role can be exercised at different levels within a team and can be easily combined with another role. As a manager a completer finisher needs to pay careful attention to their delegation skills and to keep unnecessary interference to a minimum. In a junior role a completer finisher will need to develop tact and discretion so as to avoid earning a reputation as a 'nit picker and worrier'. Completer finishers also tend to possess a nervous drive that needs to be controlled and directed if it is to have positive results.

The following page provides a summary of the various characteristics of the Belbin Types.

Belbin team types summary

Type	Typical features	Positive qualities	Allowable weaknesses
Company worker/ imple- mentor	Solid, dependable, predicable and reliable	Organizing ability, practical common sense, hard working, self discipline	Lack of flexibility, unresponsiveness to unproven ideas. Concern to maintain the status quo on efficiency
Chair/ co-ordinator	Steady, patient, self confident, controlled, commands respect	Puts people at ease. Able to get people working together. Good at standing back. A strong sense of objectives and task achievements	Not necessarily the best at thinking radically or creatively

Type	Typical features	Positive qualities	Allowable weaknesses
Shaper	Energetic, outgoing, tense, dynamic, egotistic	Drive and readiness to make things happen. Challenges ineffectiveness, complacency or self-deception	Prone to provocation, irritation and impatience. Can be selfish in terms of satisfying self first
Plant	Individualistic, serious-minded, unorthodox	Genius, imagination, intellect, knowledge. Concerned with the Big Issues	Up in the clouds, inclined to disregard practical details or protocol. Wrapped up with own ideas
Resource investigator	Extroverted, enthusiastic, curious, communicative	A capacity for contacting people and exploring anything new. An ability to respond to challenges and harness resources. Able to sell ideas and excite people	Liable to lose interest once the initial fascination has passed. Needs to be kept focused
Monitor evaluator	Unemotional, cautious, rational and analytical	Judgement, discretion, hard-headedness. Does things right	Lacks inspiration or the ability to activate others. Over concerned with getting things right
Team worker	Interpersonally skilled, sensitive, strong team player	An ability to respond to people and to situations, and to promote team spirit	Indecisiveness at moments of crisis. Being too kind to others or over anxious about individuals
Completer finisher	Detail oriented, conscientious, anxious	A capacity for follow through. Perfectionist. Creates urgency, provides focus	A tendency to worry about small things. A reluctance to 'let go'. Can annoy by excessive worrying

Key actions

- Consider your role preferences?

- How do they impact on your effectiveness?

- Think of your colleagues and their preferences?

- Review your team's composition?

- Consider the tasks your team has to perform?

CHAPTER EIGHT

Mastering time management

Mastering time management

Managing time

Most of us like to project a workplace image of being very busy and hardworking but all too often we fail to really examine the results of our ceaseless energy and activity. At the same time we will often complain about not having enough time to do things in our day-to-day lives. This problem often stems from the fact that we fail to manage our time as ruthlessly as we might. Frequently we fall into the trap of not focusing on our real priorities. As such, we allow less important activities to distract us from what is really important to our success. As a result the urgent short-term issues drive out our important, strategic issues. Many of us might respond to this argument by asserting that our time management problems are often the fault of other peoples' behaviour, constant inter-ruptions, lengthy meetings, overly complex reporting requirements and so on. Whilst there may be some truth in these factors many good managers are nonetheless able to overcome such obstacles. By simple analysis, planning and self discipline we are all capable of saving a consid-erable amount of time each day. This means managing and redirecting our time to more focused and planned purposes.

In managing our time we should consider two main elements:

1 Routine time

This is the time we use to manage our day-to-day activities, e.g. e-mail, staff meetings, administration etc.

2 Defensible time

This is the time we use for dealing with our real priorities, e.g. thinking, strategic planning, budgeting, customer or client meetings.

DELEGATION

Delegate anything that other people can do:

- **Better than you.** Are you taking advantage of people who have more knowledge and experience of you in aspects of your role?

- **At less cost than you.** Are you using your time effectively given what you earn? Are there other people who could do the work at a lower cost to your organization?

- **As part of their development and training.** If you are having to do something that you think someone else should be doing, then you may well have identified a training need for that person. Use the situation to develop their skills and capabilities.

- **As part of their normal work load.** Is it possible to pass activities on to other people as part of their day-to-day activities? Are you holding on to things that other people could do?

Remember to delegate authority as well as responsibility and resist the temptation to hang on to all the interesting jobs yourself.

Managing your time effectively

BE CLEAR ABOUT YOUR OBJECTIVES

- Are you allocating sufficient attention to your current activities, reviewing past performance and future planning? In particular, are you devoting sufficient time to planning for the future?

- Are you allocating your time correctly between different aspects of your job? Are there any parts of your job on which you are spending too much time?

- Who are the people you ought to be allocating time to? Are you spending sufficient time with them?

CONSIDER YOUR WORK

- Do you organize your working day and week according to your priorities? Or do you deal with problems as and when they occur without stopping to think if there is something more important that you should be focusing on?

- Are you able to complete tasks uninterrupted or are you constantly interrupted? Are the interruptions an essential part of your work or part of your own making?

- Are you certain that you are not working on tasks or issues that you could delegate? Remember, many people say they could do more if they were only allowed to by their managers.

Try considering the following as potential targets for managing your time. How possible would it be for you to achieve them?

- Reduce your working week by ten hours.

- Reduce daily interruptions by 50%.

- Reduce the time you spend on phone calls by 50%.

- Reduce the time you spend on e-mail and correspondence by 30%.

- Double the time you allocate to planning and thinking.

- Allocate at least 30 minutes each day for quality thinking.

Tackling 'time robbers'

A time robber is something that prevents us from completing more important and productive tasks. Time robbers are activities that absorb lots of time without producing equivalent benefit for the efforts employed. Interruptions, lengthy meetings and routine tasks (that could be delegated) are some of the most common time robbers we have to face. To control time robbers we need to employ techniques such as avoiding the activity, shortening the time we spend on it, or simply eliminating it altogether. The following is a list of classic time robbers. Review the list and highlight those you have difficulty with.

	Big problem for me	Often a problem	Seldom a problem
Planning and organizing			
1 Not setting SMART objectives			
2 Failing to plan my time on a daily basis			
3 Unclear or changing priorities			
4 Leaving tasks unfinished			
5 Crisis Management – too much 'fire fighting'			
6 Poor self-discipline			
7 Over-stretching myself – setting unrealistic targets			
8 Lack of organization/untidy desk – too much paperwork			
9 Lack of clear responsibility and authority			
10 Too many people reporting to me or that I have to report to			
11 Taking on too much myself			
12 Getting too involved in routine detail that I don't need to			
13 Not delegating enough to my team			
14 Lacking the motivation to do anything about it			
15 Inability to say 'no' to others			
16 Not coping with change			
17 Too many telephone interruptions			
18 Casual visitors who interupt me			

	Big problem for me	Often a problem	Seldom a problem
Planning and organizing 19 My self-discipline			
20 Getting swamped by e-mail			
21 Making mistakes that lead to work			
22 Failing to maintain standards, progress reports			
23 Incomplete information			
Communicating 24 Effectively stating my objectives at meetings			
25 Under/unclear/ over-communicating			
26 Failing to listen properly			
27 Socializing too frequently			
Decision-making 28 Snap decision-making			
29 Indecision/delaying matters too much			
30 Decision by committee			
31 Perfectionist tendencies			

Understanding your motivation

Effective time management – a checklist

1   Keep focused on your personal objectives.

2   In order not to delay or put off decisions:
   - Deal with one task at a time
   - Allocate specific times of the day for key activities, e.g. making important phone calls – call between 10:00-10:30 each day
   - Keep to your plans
   - Begin NOW, TODAY!

3   Don't destroy your good ideas with negative internal dialogue or self-talk. Think results and outcomes. Stay focused on what you want to achieve – this will help you motivate yourself on difficult tasks and steer off those that are unimportant.

4   Work smarter not harder – spend more time on the important issues, less on the urgent.

5   Avoid working in panic mode and waiting until the last minute before doing things.

6   Review your working practices regularly – should you really be doing this job?

7   Find time to do your Big Picture thinking – to think of the longer term and be creative.

8   Do you sometimes feel dis-empowered? Is this based on fact or fear? Avoid negative thoughts and focus on what you can control and take action on.

9   Establish clear timescales for completing tasks.

10 Indulge yourself, make time for breaks and plan pleasant tasks on a regular basis. Find time to enjoy your interests and hobbies.

11 Begin the day with an early success, then you are in the right frame of mind to tackle the rest of the day's challenges.

12 Instigate BANJO immediately – Bang A Nasty Job Off, every day.

Time management challenges and ideas

Classic problem	Response
Personal interruptions	Begin a process of red time appointments: • No interruptions please for the next hour! • Work in a quiet room • Operate an engaged 'keep out' notice
Telephone interruptions	• State you have 'one minute only' to deal with it • Request they call back • Say "Sorry it's not convenient at the moment" or "I can give you five minutes"
Personal organization	• Establish clear goals • Be clear as to your key result areas • Focus on your key objectives • Buy a time management organizer • Read a book on time management
E-mail and paperwork overload	• Use the 4 'D's: Delegate, Deal, Destroy, Divert
Waiting action	• Operate a time fillers file – deal with the issues in slack moments

Classic problem	Response
Never enough hours in the day	• Delegate tasks, say "NO" more often • Operate a rigorous 'To-do' list
Disorganized desk	• Operate a 'Musts', 'Shoulds' and 'Coulds' filing system • Review your in-tray twice a day – be ruthless in dealing with paper
Too many crises	• Ask why are they happening?
Meetings too long	• Operate a 60/90 minute rule • Get people to submit proposals in advance

Planning and organizing your time

On a daily basis

1   Plan tomorrow today:

- List all the things you need to do.
- Value each task, prioritize them in terms of importance and urgency.
- Complete certain tasks together, e.g. telephoning, dictating, reading.
- Calculate the time needed for each activity.
- Allocate parts of the day to deal with each group of tasks.

2   Leave part of your day free to deal with the unexpected.

3   Highlight one major objective for the day and complete it.

4   Think about what is your best time for working and complete important tasks during this period.

5   Reduce interruptions.

6   Plan a reflective 'thinking' period for part of your day.

7   Review your daily plans.

8   Remember you cannot influence the length of the working day.

9   Travel by train, it is preferable to car journeys. You can work on the way and arrive fresh.

10 Which of the following activities do you feel uncomfortable about doing:

- Sitting and thinking, however important?
- Sitting and reading, however relevant?
- Having a clear desk, however effective?

11 Do the above activities generate important results for you? If they do, why should you feel guilty?

Minimize the effects of interruptions

Dealing with office interruptions

1   Be clear as to what is more important, the task in hand or the interruption.

2   Don't get trapped into the detail of the interruption – take control and set up a separate meeting or ask them to come back later.

3   Ask your assistant to screen visitors.

4   Train your staff to say "Is now a good time?" as they interrupt or call you.

5 Specify a set time for the interruption and keep to it ("I can give you five minutes!").

6 Get people to submit a list of points in advance when they ask for an appointment so that your time is not wasted on irrelevant matters.

7 Use another office for 'thinking' or important creative work.

8 Don't be afraid to offend people, say "no" more often ("Sorry I have another urgent appointment").

9 Suggest that someone else meets the visitor.

10 Remain standing up; sitting down can lead to the interruption becoming a long meeting.

11 Whilst an open door policy represents a positive attitude it should not be interpreted literally for every minute of the day.

12 Be direct and honest with time-wasters. ("I'm sorry I don't have the time to deal with this at the moment").

Managing crises

How to reduce crises

1 Use effective diary planning to pre-empt problems.

2 Be decisive, don't leave things to the last minute.

3 Focus on your key objectives; don't get side tracked by urgent but relatively unimportant tasks or problems.

4 Remember that things normally take longer than you think; allow for this when planning.

5 What do you want to achieve? What are your expectations?

- What will happen if you don't tackle the issue sooner?

- What are the steps involved in clearing the issue from your to do list??

- What is the first step or decision you must take?

- Start actioning matters today!

6 Problem solving:

- First define the problem, not the answer.

- Emphasize your key objectives in addressing the problem.

- List all the possible solutions, be radical and creative in your thinking.

- Identify the resources available to you.

- Select the most suitable solution.

- Implement the solution.

- Review the results.

Ensuring that efficient time management is maintained

Operating a clean desk policy

1 Keep only relevant papers on your desk, the task you are currently dealing with.

2 Let other people know that you are operating a clean desk policy.

3 Deal with all papers immediately using the following guidelines:

- Action it (80% of paperwork can be dealt with immediately).

- Identify the main points and then bin or file.

4 Clear your desk at the end of each day.

5 Record actions in your diary rather than a desk file to remind you of important tasks.

6   Complete each small task before moving to another.

7   Take action sooner rather than later.

8   Use pocket recorders for speedy action and do not forget notes.

9   Do your own filing.

10 Avoid touching the same piece of paper more than once.

CHAPTER NINE

Mastering meetings

Mastering meetings

An introduction to managing meetings

We all spend a huge amount of time sitting in meetings and, when effective, they can be a very useful means of communicating between people or teams. However, all too frequently we get a poor return because we spend too much time relative to the outcomes we secure from a meeting. For any meeting to be productive we need to be absolutely clear about the objective and outcome. Whether it be to discuss a specific issue, develop alternatives, approve plans, agree actions or develop commitment it is imperative that we know this at the outset. Without this focus any meeting runs the risk of meandering and so wasting time and resources. When chairing meetings we need to ensure that everyone is clear as to the aims and objectives and that everyone attending contributes fully to the discussions.

Whilst it is vital in any meeting that we are clear about what we have to achieve, we also need to know how we are going to achieve those results. To succeed in the above we need to have some appreciation of the process side of running meetings.

Techniques for managing meetings

The process side of meetings

The skills needed to successfully run meetings involves encouraging people to contribute and at the same time controlling the discussion and keeping proceedings on track. The following behaviours help to achieve these objectives.

BEHAVIOURS TO ENCOURAGE INDIVIDUAL CONTRIBUTIONS DURING A MEETING

When chairing meetings make sure you:

- Use open-ended questions that collect information. So what are your views on this issue? How do you think we might tackle the problem?

- Use direct eye contact with the group or specific individuals. Ensure that you are speaking to each individual – eye contact ensures that you connect with everyone around the table.

- Highlight people's expertise and encourage or invite their comments into the discussion.

- Give people notice that you want them to speak, e.g. mention their name, followed by a preamble and then an open question: "I know Pierre has a view on this following his experiences with x, Pierre perhaps you would like to share your views with us?"

- Use silences to provoke input – if you stay quiet someone will eventually break the silence.

- Manage a formal sequence of contributions; ask people one after each other to comment. This stops people cross-talking and puts them on alert.

- Test understanding of issues by summarizing and asking for comments. "So it seems we are unable to hit the targets with the existing resources, how do we react to this information?"

- Build on people's suggestions or ideas; help create a positive climate around the table.

- Increase the level of the formality surrounding the meeting, e.g. "Could I ask for all comments through the chair please?"

Behaviours to avoid in chairing meetings:

- Interrupting others.

- Shutting out people or ignoring them from the discussion.

- Defending or attacking people. As a chairperson you have to be objective. If we have very strong views on a subject we should perhaps get someone else to run the meeting.

- Allowing side discussions to break out; only one person at a time should speak.

- Making judgmental comments; to avoid such behaviours ask others for their opinions before you comment.

CONTROLLING THE DIRECTION OF MEETINGS

To control the direction of a meeting use the following strategies:

- Announce how you plan to run the meeting at the beginning. This helps set expectations.

- Allocate specific times to each agenda item.

- Use short open-ended questions to guide the discussions.

- Make regular summaries.

- Use open-ended questions on any new subject areas that need to be discussed.

- Use direct questions towards people who meander in their comments: "So what is the exact point you are making?"

CHANGING THE PACE OF MEETINGS

Your opening statement will influence the pace of any meeting. A long and slowly delivered introduction will set the tone for a slow meeting. Conversely, a focused and fast paced introduction is likely to be followed by a faster moving and more effective meeting.

Review progress during the meeting to help generate energy and increase the pace. Try, "How do people feel we are progressing – do we need to move faster?" You can also inject more energy into a meeting by being more animated and putting more variation in your voice tone.

Successful meetings are ones that not only achieve objectives but do so in an effective way. As a chairperson it is your function to achieve results using the most appropriate process. You can use a wide range of behaviours to achieve this. The above lists give some of the more commonly used behaviours. With such a wide range of behaviours available to help you direct your meetings it is possible to successfully run them without using the formal power of the chair's role.

Controlling forceful or dominant characters in a meeting

In any meeting we will at sometime or other need to manage strong characters. Taking control in such circumstances is the sign of an effective chair and the strategies listed below can help you to manage difficult characters.

- Ask closed questions to prevent them giving protracted answers or making lengthy speeches. For example, "So can you simply confirm whether you are in agreement or not with the question?"

- Breaking eye contact with someone can indicate that you want to move onto other people.

- By using outward hand gestures you can signal that you want the difficult person to conclude their comments or observations. This can be enforced by a tactful or diplomatic comment such as, "Thank you for that contribution Jean" as you signal your desire for them to finish.

- Interrupting and skilfully summarizing can control proceedings and at the same time inject a greater sense of urgency.

- Introduce greater formality: if you anticipate a lively meeting, introducing a more formal tone can help to control proceedings. The use of formal titles can also raise the sense of formality, e.g. "Mr. Johnson, I'd like to ask a question."

- Switch the conversation to other team members either by directed questions or by shifting your eye contact to the person you want to bring into the discussion.

Managing the classic disruptive characters at meetings

THE FOOTBALL TERRACE SUPPORTER

Likes to attack and antagonize others. Aggressive in their approach and voice tone.

Strategies: appeal to the rest of the group – isolate them: "Do we all agree with the comment?" Institutionalize the role: comment that it's helpful to have a devil's advocate position.

THE EXPERT

Likes to help but keeps interrupting with long explanations or providing lots of detail.

Strategies: appeal to their nature, "Can you help me to control matters by carrying out a specific role during the meeting? Can you take a note of the issues we miss or fail to recognize?"

THE INTROVERT

Says nothing, stays removed from the proceedings even though their input is necessary.

Strategies: ask directed questions to them, "So Julie do you have a view on this point?"

THE DETAIL FREAK

Likes to promote themselves as the guardians of all wisdom and truth during the meeting. Willing to concentrate on the details and point out any inconsistencies in the discussion.

Strategies: point out the need to simplify issues for preliminary discussion then record their comments. Discuss their issues during a coffee break and ask for advice on how to address them. Get them to comment on the points during the reconvened meeting.

THE DOODLER

The potential day dreamer.

Strategies: don't intervene, but if the behaviour is distracting to others then again try to harness their inputs by the use of direct questions.

THE PASSIVE INTERRUPTER

Generates side-discussions with colleagues so resulting in disruptive behaviour.

Strategies: intervene promptly to tackle the behaviour: "Is there a problem or issue?" or "Anything you want to share with the rest of the group?"or "Could we have one meeting at a time please!"

How to make your meetings more productive

- Ask yourself is the meeting really necessary? Are there other ways in which you could achieve your objectives?

- Are your objectives in holding the meeting:
    - To make a decision?
    - To communicate key plans or new developments?
    - To review progress on an issue?
    - To generate new ideas (brainstorming type sessions)?
    - To develop a consensus?

- Produce an agenda with clear objectives.

- An ideal meeting time duration is 10 - 60 minutes maximum.

- The ideal time for starting a meeting is after 11.00am.

- Keep the number of participants attending as small as possible. The ideal number of participants is seven.

- Communicate the meeting's objectives, time and location to participants.

- Ask people to prepare or send information to the meeting in advance. Make sure you also provide adequate notice of this requirement.

- Start the meeting on time and finish on time.

- Get to the point: start with what's important.

- Keep to the agenda: we all like meetings to be managed in a fair but firm manner.

- Encourage people to leave the meeting when their involvement is no longer required.

- Use presentational aids to encourage interest and participation.

- Prevent interruptions from other people.

- If you find a meeting to be slow in pace so will others, so advise the chair of this.

- As the chairperson, summarize at key stages and signpost when the proceedings are going to move on to another topic or subject area.

- Avoid 'any other business' sections as they are usually a substitute for poor preparation.

- Question whether you need to get into the game of taking elaborate minutes or notes. They are often a substitute for 'cover your arse!' type cultures. A simple decision or action sheet is much more useful.

- Should your meeting be held standing up? Stand up meetings can seriously reduce time wasting behaviours and are ideal for short focused meetings that require prompt action. When people sit down they get comfortable and that can mean spending more time discussing matters.

CHAPTER TEN

Mastering the skills of assertion

Mastering the skills of assertion

The difference between passive, assertive and aggressive behaviour

Passive behaviour

Passive behaviour is often described as being apathetic or unresponsive to others. Passive behaviour means you do not assert your own rights and is often characterized by the perspective of 'I lose, you win'. This may also result in feelings of being victimized and perhaps landing the rough end of a deal. In effect passive behaviour ensures that we don't stand up for what we want or believe in.

Aggressive behaviour

In contrast, aggressive behaviour involves adopting a threatening or domineering attitude and frequently results in a 'I win, you lose' perspective. Passive or unassertive people can easily fall victim to aggressive behaviour.

Aggressive behaviour often involves putting someone down though the use of anger and hurtful statements. The purpose of aggressive behaviour is to damage or attack the integrity of someone else. So ridicule or humiliation is a vital component of aggressive behaviour. So why do some people adopt such behaviours? Well there are many possible reasons that might help explain it such as:

- A simple lack of knowledge or awareness of other more effective influencing behaviours. "I only know one way to get things done and that is by shouting at people!"

- A genuine lack of human insight and sensitivity towards others. Some people do not realize the impact of their behaviour on others or if they do they choose to simply ignore it. This might lead some individuals to be described as arrogant or selfish.

- An inflated and egocentric personality can often result in unreasonable and excessively demanding behaviours that can tip into aggressive postures: "I am right and you're wrong."

- Feelings of powerlessness and low self esteem. Extremely aggressive behaviours can often be the result of an individual's negative feelings about themself. Lacking a positive self image might cause some people to hide behind an aggressive exterior that they might mistakenly confuse with strength and confidence.

- A fear of being threatened by others: "By getting my retaliation in first I retain my strength."

- Past experiences might cause some people to react aggressively. In situations where they may have been felt weakened they may want to assert their rights by aggressive behaviour.

The consequences of aggressive behaviour can be:

- A sense of satisfaction from the immediate release and assertion that the person is in control: "I told them who was boss today. Nobody was left in any doubt who was in charge!"

- Feelings of achievement in satisfying short-term needs: "I really screwed them down on the price to get the deal I wanted."

- Retaliation in the long run. People who are on the end of aggressive behaviour normally resort to finding ways in which they can get their own back in the long-term. Aggressive behaviour does tend to generate enemies.

- Defensiveness on the part of the individual. Aggressive behaviour normally limits rather than promotes dialogue between two people.

- Sub-optimal results. In the long run aggressive behaviour will generate results that fall short of what could have been achieved by a more collaborative and productive approach.

Assertive behaviour

Assertive behaviour is a major approach to enhancing our influencing skills. Assertion skills are based on some fundamental principles. These principles are often referred to as the Bill of Rights and they form the building blocks of assertive behaviour:

- I have the right to exist.

- I have the right to state my own needs and wants.

- I have the right to be treated with respect.

- I have the right to express my own feelings, values and opinions.

- I have the right to say yes or no for myself.

- I have the right to make mistakes.

- I have the right to change my own mind.

- I have the right to say I do not understand.

- I have the right to decline responsibility for other people's problems.

- I have the right to deal with others without having to depend on their approval.

These rights in turn have implications for how we interact and deal with others. These can be best expressed by the following:

- Everybody has their own personal space.

- We do not have the right to invade another person's space without invitation.

- We don't have the right to manipulate others.

- Other people have the choice as to whether or not they want to respond to us.

People who are assertive seek to be authentic and rational in all their dealings with others. They also want to 'own' any problem they are dealing with and not push them onto someone else. Assertive people are not afraid to express their feelings and emotions to influence others.

Assertive behaviour allows us to express our needs in simple but direct terms. The guiding principle being to be fair to oneself and to respect others.

The benefits of assertive behaviour are:

- A greater sense of self-respect and individual identity.
- Increased self confidence.
- Greater mental and physical well-being: reduced stress and anxiety at work.
- Optimizing personal potential.

Behaving assertively

Assertive behaviours demand that we:

- Tell other people what we want.
- Protect our needs.
- Avoid being manipulated by others.
- Seck clarification of other people's requests.
- Confront problems as soon as possible.

Assertiveness techniques

Use 'I' statements and avoid the use of 'We', 'One' and 'You'. The use of 'I' is much more forceful than hiding behind the company or the boss or the team. When you want something 'I' is much more influential.

At the same time keep your comments and statements short and to the point. Avoid the tendency in difficult situations to over elaborate which often provides people with other cues to latch onto.

If the discussions get heated always remain calm and keep your voice tone low and moderated.

Assertive behaviour recognizes the basic rights that we all have and is a way of allowing us to be persuasive whilst resisting aggressive or manipulative behaviours. Equally, assertiveness is not a form of manipulation but rather a skill that allows us to express ourselves openly and forcefully. In learning assertive behaviour we must first buy into the rights associated with the behaviours.

Using assertive techniques to give feedback

Different types of assertive behaviour have been developed and one very useful approach involves the process of giving feedback. Giving feedback in an assertive manner focuses on three critical areas:

- The specific behaviour under discussion.

- The expression of feelings surrounding the situation.

- The impact of the behaviour under discussion.

THE SPECIFIC BEHAVIOUR UNDER DISCUSSION

This is a clear description of the behaviour that has generated the problem. When commenting be specific and avoid any generalizations or judgments about the behaviour. Simply describe the observed behaviour.

"We agreed that during the negotiations with the customer we would stick to the existing pricing policy and you ignored that agreement half way through the meeting without discussing it or clearing it with me before hand!"

THE EXPRESSION OF FEELINGS SURROUNDING THE SITUATION

In many work situations the expression of personal feelings or too much emotion is often thought to be a sign of weakness or a lack of professionalism. Yet the forceful expression of emotion or feelings can have a really powerful impact on others. Assertive people are comfortable in expressing their feelings as a way of reinforcing their needs. For example, "I am very angry and annoyed that you did not deliver the project as we had previously agreed."

In order to express our feelings we need to first identify the precise feelings that have been aroused by a specific behaviour. There is no value in simply reacting in a hysterical manner. So we have to be clear about what has happened and why it has impacted on us before we project our feelings.

Expressing our true feelings and emotions can also help us to reduce our stress levels since it prevents the 'storing up' of negative thoughts and worries. Equally when we analyze our true feelings in any given situation we may find out that we are in fact overreacting and that we can easily live with the behaviour.

THE IMPACT OF THE BEHAVIOUR UNDER DISCUSSION

When talking to someone about the impact of their behaviour we need to be focused on the impact, rather than the 'possibilities or risks' associated with the behaviour. This distinction helps us to identify the specific sources of our annoyance and so possibly prevent us from over reacting. No matter how well a message is presented to someone it always has the potential to cause an emotional reaction.

As well as giving feedback, assertive behaviour also helps us in receiving feedback from others. When facing difficult or aggressive situations we can all react emotionally. Whilst some people will 'fight back' and escalate the problem, others will simply accept the feedback passively without asserting their views or opinions.

FOGGING

Fogging is a classic assertiveness technique that enables us to receive negative feedback without necessarily agreeing with the comments being made. By avoiding any emotional reactions we are in a better position to receive the available feedback so that we can evaluate it and at a later stage, and in a less emotionally charged atmosphere, decide how we want to respond to it.

Typical phrases that employ fogging technique might include:

"I can see that."

"I can understand that."

"I can see you're upset about this."

"I can see why that would annoy you."

"I can accept that."

The purpose of such statements is to express acceptance and under-standing of the other point of view, without necessarily accepting responsibility for the possible cause or any future solution. In certain situations the feedback given to us may not be intended to be useful, but may be simply designed to provoke an emotional reaction. When facing these types of situations we can use some of the following techniques:

NEGATIVE ASSERTION

This technique involves using specific open-ended questions to identify the exact nature of the feedback that is being given to you. It forces the giver to identify the specific behaviour that has caused the problem.

"So you think the report is rubbish! Could you help me understand what it is precisely about the report that makes you think it is rubbish?"

EXHAUSTING THE CRITICISM

This technique uses an open-ended questioning approach to exhaust any negative feedback or complaints.

"Is there anything else about the work you don't like?"

"I understand that issue, is there anything else that you want to add or say?"

"So are there any other factors that mean you do not like the approach I have adopted?"

Negative assertion is not intended to reject feedback but is a method of dealing with ineffective feedback by converting it into more useful and helpful information that you can act on. By asking for, or stimulating constructive criticism, you help others to express their honest and negative feelings directly to you and so improve the communication flow. This approach can also assist in exposing any manipulative or invalid criticisms.

A quick guide to developing assertiveness skills

Using the techniques of negative inquiry

- Turn the attention on yourself, not your critic. By using expressions such as "What is it about me that's wrong," you avoid focusing on your critic, which often generates a defensive reaction that then escalates rather than improves a situation. So draw the feedback to yourself and don't react to the individual but use their energy to get them to focus on you. Drain them of their negative energy by simply absorbing it.

- Invite criticism or feedback. You will extract feelings from others more effectively if you convey the message, "I'm very eager to hear this valuable information. I want to know more. What don't you like about my approach?"

- Identify the specific comments or observations surrounding any criticism. Listen closely to the words being used and help your critic focus on exactly what is wrong.

  Q "You say this report is rubbish? What is it about the report that is rubbish?"

  A "Well, your structure, for one thing."

  Q "What is it about my structure that is rubbish?"

  A "Well just look at it. You haven't listed the key conclusions."

  Q "Then it's my conclusions not being clearly defined that makes the report look rubbish?"

  Q "OK – that's one thing.'"

- Exhaust the criticism.

  Q "Is there anything else about my report that is wrong?" Or, "There must be more things about the report that is wrong than just my conclusion." Or, "Are you sure there's nothing else that's wrong with the report?"

- Analyze the criticism.

  Q "What is it about ... that's wrong?"

- Listen for the 'I' statement. Remember that criticism often comes from someone else's value system, that they are often unaware that their subjective value system is operating, and that behind every piece of criticism is a statement that "I don't like it".

- Specify what your critic wants. You might make unwarranted assumptions if you don't do this.

  Q "It sounds like you want me to clear things with you before I submit my report?"

  A "Yes ... well no. Go ahead and make the decision. Just be sure to let me know as soon as possible. It's when I don't know that you've done it that I have problems."

You now have more information on which to act and manage this person.

Admitting to mistakes without beating yourself up

Often we attack ourselves for making errors. To avoid this we need to accept valid criticism without letting it escalate. Non-assertive people cope with mistakes but they can be manipulated by others through feelings of guilt or anxiety. The result is that they:

- Repeatedly seek forgiveness for making mistakes and try to make up for them.

- Alternatively, they deny the error by being defensive and engage in counter criticism, which provides hostile critics with a target on which to work out their aggressive feelings or frustration.

In either case the non-assertive person copes poorly and ultimately feels worse.

As with most of the beliefs we learned in childhood, few of us can actively change our belief that errors make us feel guilty by simply thinking about it. We must first change the way we behave and what we say to ourselves when dealing with an error so that we can react more positively to any criticism.

So how then do you cope assertively with errors? The easiest way is to simply view them as errors, no more or less, errors are just errors. In other words, you assertively accept which errors are negative about yourself. For example, when you are confronted with a critical or possibly hostile comment when making an error you can assertively accept the fact of the error by saying:

"I've forgotten to bring the keys to let us in – what a stupid mistake. What's the best thing to do now?"

This approach stops you getting into lengthy justifications as to how it was you came to forget the keys and more importantly, focuses on how you can best solve the difficulty. Other examples might entail statements such as:

"I'm sorry, I did not make a very good job of that report, you're quite right."

"I'm afraid it simply slipped my memory, I'm sorry it has made it so difficult for you, would it help if I ...?"

"I hadn't realized I kept interrupting you, I know it's a really annoying habit – I'll try to be more aware of what I'm doing in the future."

By agreeing with and accepting valid criticism, you acknowledge your mistake: remembering that you have a right to make mistakes without accepting any generalized accusations or sweeping judgments of your personality. Thus you maintain your self-esteem.

Using the broken record technique

Once you are clear about what you want, be prepared to repeat your need over and over again. This will help you to maintain your position in the face of manipulative comments, irrelevant logic or argumentative comments.

"Yes I realize you have other commitments but as we previously agreed I must have the report tomorrow morning at 9.30am. Yes, I realize the difficulties but I have to have the report at 9.30. Tomorrow morning at 9.30!"

By simply repeating your need – like a broken record – and not over elaborating or siding with the other person's needs they will soon accept your requirement.

The fogging technique

Fogging as we have already discussed is a technique that enables you to absorb another person's views, anger or hostility without reacting in any other way than simply acknowledging what they are saying. In effect you give them nothing back to escalate the anger or debate. This is a particularly useful technique in situations where we may want to simply let the other person get the issue off their chest.

Fogging might sound like:

- Yes, I can see why you are annoyed.

- I fully appreciate how you feel.

- I quite understand your anger.

By acknowledging what the other person is saying without responding specifically you can maintain your own needs without feeling defensive, aggressive or anxious. Fogging means not giving the other person something back to get further annoyed or angry.

Dealing with unjust criticism

Quite often if we are criticized by someone we develop feelings of guilt or insecurity. We may become defensive and begin to make excuses or we may involve ourselves in an argument which gets us nowhere.

By using the fogging technique and some other rules we can also deal with manipulative criticism. This approach enables us to have a defence against those who may try to influence us to behave in a certain way by using unjust criticism. By using this technique we can create situations which make it impossible for the other person to have any success. It should, of course, not be used where any criticism is valid. Whilst acknowledging that there may be some truth in what someone says, you essentially remain your own judge of what you do as a result. This allows you to receive criticism without becoming anxious or defensive, while giving no rewards to those attempting to apply criticism that is manipulative.

In addition to the use of fogging, the technique involves applying a few other simple rules can also be used:

- Don't deny any criticism – if you do you are providing the other person with more ammunition.

- Don't become defensive – if you do you are admitting that the criticism may be justified.

- Don't respond by counter criticism – this may escalate matters and start an argument.

- DO LISTEN – and respond using the same words.

- Respond ONLY to what the critic actually says, not to what they imply.

Examples of statements that can be used include:

- "You may be right."

- "I can understand why you think that."

- "That's a point. You obviously feel strongly about the matter."

Calling time out

Calling time out is a powerful technique that allows you to buy time to think about a situation and respond in a more considered manner at a later time. Often we can be placed into a difficult situation by people almost jumping on us and demanding an immediate response. This often puts us off guard and what assertive people are good at is finding the time to gather their thoughts in a controlled manner. The response can be a simple:

"I understand that you have to deal with an angry customer, however, at this exact moment in time I do not have all the background or information to respond properly. If you can let me have ten to fifteen minutes then I will get back to you on these points."

You will observe that the response is very considered and reasonable. It acknowledges the person's plight and gives a real commitment to respond in a set time. Of course this might vary depending on the circumstances from a few minutes to one week. But often people rely on us dropping everything to deal with their issues regardless of our needs. Calling time out is a simple way of asserting your rights to get the correct information in order to respond. It can be very effective in dealing with people who barge into your office demanding immediate satisfaction. It can also help in dealing with irate customers. Clearly, however, you must get back to people, otherwise you will have an even bigger problem when they return. Again, assertiveness involves commitments on your behalf. It is NOT a technique for getting rid of difficult tasks.

Learning to say 'no!'

We all find ourselves in situations where we may be trying to make a point but the other person seems intent on avoiding or ignoring our request. When another person fails to accept your answer or request and resorts to pressure tactics you need to handle the situation in a more assertive way. We do this by simply choosing a phrase or statement that we feel comfortable with, and without getting angry or loud we simply repeat the statement (as indicated in our broken record approach) each time the other person tries another form of manipulation to persuade you to change your mind.

By staying focused on our statement and resisting the temptation to answer, or respond to attacks or insults, we can eventually convince the other person that we are not prepared to be ignored or diverted, for example:

- "I can't work late this evening."

- "I don't think you heard me, I'm not able to work this evening."

- "Let me say it again, I'm not able to work this evening."

- "That's really irrelevant to the main issue, which is that I'm not able to work this evening."

This broken record use of the assertive 'no' will eventually get heard as it is uncomfortable to listen to for too long. It really is an effective way of saying 'no' in difficult situations and can provide you with a greater sense of confidence and deal with the anxiety you might have.

Using empathy

When saying 'no' to people we need to be careful that there is no confusion between refusing a request and rejecting the person. Some people fall into this trap and confuse a 'no' as a rejection of them. By employing empathy with people we can soften the 'no' side of any refusal.

This is easily achieved by simply reflecting back to the other person their request but adding, "I'm sorry, I can't do that". This helps to show that you have listened to the request and that you do empathize, for example, "I really understand your problem about completing the work urgently but I'm not able to work this evening because of a previous commitment." We are in effect trying to sympathize with the other person's difficulty but at the same time asserting our needs – whereas a flat 'no' can send a more aggressive message of 'I don't care' which may not be effective for developing long-term relationships.

Promote workable compromises

This technique often needs to be combined with the 'how to say no' technique. On hearing of the 'broken record, no' technique some people will rightly argue that wandering around their organization flatly refusing to help people will result in their swift exit from the organization – and they are probably right. So it is important to realize that assertiveness is not about behaving in an unco-operative way or manner. A key part of assertiveness skills involves seeking alternative options or compromises.

If someone won't give in and is being equally assertive with you it is often appropriate to offer a compromise to both parties (remembering that your goals include self-respect, not necessarily getting your own way and defending yourself, rather than allowing yourself to be put down). When your self respect is not in question try offering a compromise that may work for both parties, for example, "I can't work late this evening but as it is important, I'm prepared to come in early tomorrow."

In most situations we can manage the situation more effectively by better using the 'How to say no' technique along with empathy and a genuine willingness to look for a workable compromise. Assertiveness is not about rejecting people, it involves a requirement on the individual to seek out satisfactory outcomes for both parties.

Eight essential tips in behaving assertively

1 NEVER HIT BELOW THE BELT

Verbal blows below the belt are unfair. We all have certain areas that are sensitive to us and if these are breached we cannot be expected to respond rationally. The effect of hitting below the belt is to cause hurt and resentment and puts any working relationship in danger. Such strategies are normally the domain of the bully.

2 DON'T PLAY GAMES

Don't pretend to go along with something or agree to it when you don't intend to follow through. Equally don't pretend to be something you are not. Stay true to yourself and be honest in your dealings with others. Assertiveness is about being genuine and authentic in all your dealings.

3 DON'T PLAY THE AMATEUR PSYCHOLOGIST

None of us has the ability to read the mind of another person. All the information we have about people involves what we can see in terms of their behaviour. Nothing angers someone more than telling them what they are 'really' thinking, or what they are 'really' like, and what is causing their behaviour. So stick to commenting on what people do and not what you think they are thinking!

4 AVOID STEREOTYPING

No one likes being boxed or labelled. We all want to be regarded as individuals. Stereotyping someone has the potential to cause resentment. Deal with people as individuals and avoid labelling them as types. For example, cone heads, digit heads etc.

5 AVOID 'PIGGY BANKING'

Don't let minor grievances pass without comment. Avoid waiting until you have a whole piggy bank full of irritations and grievances. The danger is that one 'last straw' mistake may cause your full piggy bank to burst, creating a spilling out of all past resentments and making a huge issue out of a small one. If someone does something that annoys you deal with it promptly – don't save it for a rainy day.

6 FORGET THE PAST AND WORK ON THE FUTURE

Don't live in the past and dig into history. The past cannot be changed – it can only be learnt from. Try to focus on the future and work in the 'here and now'.

7 AVOID GENERALIZATIONS

Generalizing statements about people such as "You always.." or "You never.." are pointless and accomplish little. Assertive behaviour demands that we are specific about the comments we make of others.

8 DON'T GO BALLISTIC

Do not use techniques of overkill. Do not threaten extreme sanctions for minor mistakes or errors. In overreacting to situations you only weaken your credibility and case.

Neutralizing anger

In angry situations we may well need to try to reduce our feelings of aggression so that we:

- Feel more comfortable.

- Begin to listen.

- Can begin to try to solve the problem together.

When someone is criticizing us or is involved in a personal attack against us and we want to confront the problem rather than escape, fight or pretend there is not a problem, then it is important to neutralize any feelings of anger. We might consider using the following technique with a boss, friend, colleague or any other person in authority who is engaged in attacking us.

The action steps for neutralizing anger

1 Recognize the anger being displayed: "I can see you are very angry."

2 Express your desire to solve the problem(s): "I want to hear what you have to say. Let's try and work this out together."

3 Get the angry person to lower their voice and sit down by using a normal voice and a calming tone: "Why don't you sit down and see if we can talk about what's happened. I really want to go through this issue."

4   Use the skills of active listening to hear all the complaints before moving into any problem-solving mode: "It sounds like this has been irritating you for a long time. This last incident must have seemed like the end."

In some situations it can help to admit early on the possibility that you might have been part of the problem:

"Maybe I could have arrived earlier."

"I want to hear what you have to say. Perhaps I made a mistake."

This way of approaching anger naturally assumes we are willing to handle the problem and move beyond active listening to try to resolve the problem. If we are simply trying to placate the other person this may well lead to further conflict. We have to be serious about solving the issue.

CHAPTER ELEVEN

Summary checklists

Summary checklists

Are you a leader or a ****

Leader	****
Carries things for people	Gets other people to carry things
Appeals to the best in people; opens doors; provides guidance. Is a cheerleader to people	Is anonymous and invisible – expects instructions to be carried out without question
Thinks of ways to empower people to greater productivity and rewards. Is focused on company goals	Thinks of personal rewards, status and how they look to outsiders
At ease with people – values them	Uncomfortable/strained – uses people for their own agenda
Removes parking places and other executive privileges	Has perks in abundance – actively encourages them
Goes where people want them	Sits where they want to
Good listener	Good talker
Uncompromising on personal/ company values	Values are nice to haves

Leader	****
Available	Hard to reach
Firm but fair with all	Fair to a favoured few; exploits the rest
Decisive	Indecisive – uses committees, bureaucracy
Ego in place	Egotistical and arrogant in equal amounts
Tough – confronts difficult problems head on	Elusive – avoids tough issues
Persistent and determined	Surrenders and gives up easily
Simplifies (makes it look easy)	Complicates (makes it look difficult)
Tolerant of open disagreement / conflict	Intolerant of open disagreement / conflict
Knows people's names	Doesn't know people's names
Has strong convictions	Convictions can be expensive!
Does dog-work when necessary	Is above doing any kind of dog-work
Trusts people	Trusts only words and numbers

Leader	****
Delegates important jobs	Retains control – micro manager
Wants personal anonymity but publicity for his company	Self-serving – "I/Me" agenda dominates
Often takes the blame	Looks for a scapegoat
Gives credit to others	Takes all the credit; complains about lack of good people
Gives honest, frequent feedback	Talks behind people – plays games
Knows when and how to fire people with dignity	Avoids unpleasant people tasks or does them very badly
Goes to help where there is a problem	Interrupts people in crisis and calls them to meetings in their office
Respects people	"Most people are lazy and incompetent"
Knows the business and the kind of people who make it tick	They've never met
Honest under pressure	Two faced – says one thing and does another
Looks to abolish controls	Loves introducing controls

Leader	****
Prefers face to face contact instead of memos	Prefers memos, long reports, written communications
Straightforward	Tricky and manipulative
Consistent and credible to people	Unpredictable; says what they think people want to hear
Admits own mistakes; comforts others when they admit them	Allegedly never makes mistakes; blames others; starts witch hunts to identify culprits
No policy manuals	Policy manuals are rife
Openness	Secrecy

How is management in your organization?

(Adapted from an idea originally contained in Tom Peters and Nancy Austins' 'A Passion For Excellence', Collins 1985.)

Absolute don'ts for real leaders

1   Don't abuse people.

2   Don't make people feel weak.

3   Don't talk at people all the time.

4   Don't devalue people or simply 'use' them.

5   Don't deny responsibility.

6   Don't avoid risk.

7   Don't avoid people problems.

8   Don't gloss over issues.

9   Don't de-motivate.

10 Don't be negative.

11 Don't be reactive.

12 Don't be lazy.

13 Don't always insist on perfection.

14 Don't resist change.

15 Don't be pessimistic.

16 Don't tell lies.

17 Don't be indecisive.

18 Don't lose sight of your goals/aims.

19 Don't be inconsistent.

Listening

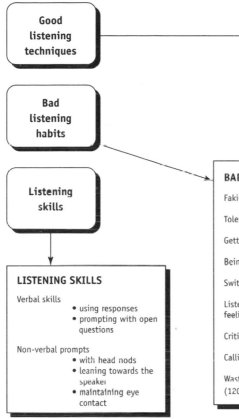

Good listening techniques

Bad listening habits

Listening skills

GOOD LISTENING TECHNIQUES

Using questions or comments that focus on what was said

Requesting clarification of points

Restating the message (paraphrasing)

Neutral response

Reflective response – so you think X?

Positive response – I like the idea

BAD LISTENING HABITS

Faking attention

Tolerating or creating distractions

Getting over excited and losing the point

Being thrown by emotive words

Switching-off from discussing difficult things

Listening only for facts and not the ideas or feelings behind the issue

Criticizing the speaker's ability/prose/accent

Calling the subject matter uninteresting

Wasting the differential between speaking rate (120 wpm) and the listening rate (400 wpm)

LISTENING SKILLS

Verbal skills
- using responses
- prompting with open questions

Non-verbal prompts
- with head nods
- leaning towards the speaker
- maintaining eye contact

Feedback

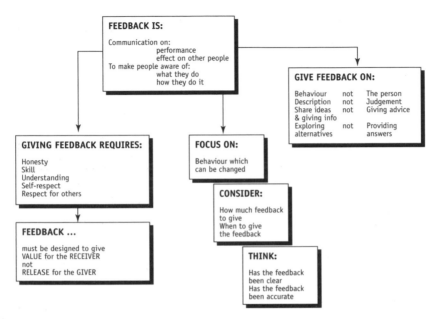

FEEDBACK IS:

Communication on:
        performance
        effect on other people
To make people aware of:
        what they do
        how they do it

GIVE FEEDBACK ON:

Behaviour	not	The person
Description	not	Judgement
Share ideas & giving info	not	Giving advice
Exploring alternatives	not	Providing answers

GIVING FEEDBACK REQUIRES:

Honesty
Skill
Understanding
Self-respect
Respect for others

FOCUS ON:

Behaviour which
can be changed

CONSIDER:

How much feedback
to give
When to give
the feedback

FEEDBACK ...

must be designed to give
VALUE for the RECEIVER
not
RELEASE for the GIVER

THINK:

Has the feedback
been clear
Has the feedback
been accurate

Delegation

What is delegation?

Delegation varies in degree from 'instruction' to 'abdication'.

Delegation can be defined as:

> *'Giving someone the freedom and authority to handle certain matters on their own initiative – with the confidence that they can do the job successfully.'*

How should you delegate?

Before delegation

- Select the right staff.

- Train and develop them.

- Plan what is to be delegated.

When delegating	• Tell the person
	– what has to be done – the task
	– why it has to be done
	– what results are required
	– what timescales and quality standards are required.
	• Tell others
	– what authority has been given.
When the task is being completed	• Check progress at agreed stages.
	• Help only if asked.
After the task	• Provide constructive feedback.

A simple guide to managing performance

Key results areas (KRAS)	Performance standards (Time, cost, quality)
1	
2	
3	
4	
5	
6	
7	

Objectives to be achieved	Action steps to achieve objectives
Area of responsibility: *(Use key action verbs)* Objective: Target Date:	
Area of responsibility: Objective: Target Date:	
Area of responsibility: Objective: Target Date:	
Area of responsibility: Objective: Target Date:	
Personal development area: Objective:	

A short guide to making better use of your time

Ask yourself these questions

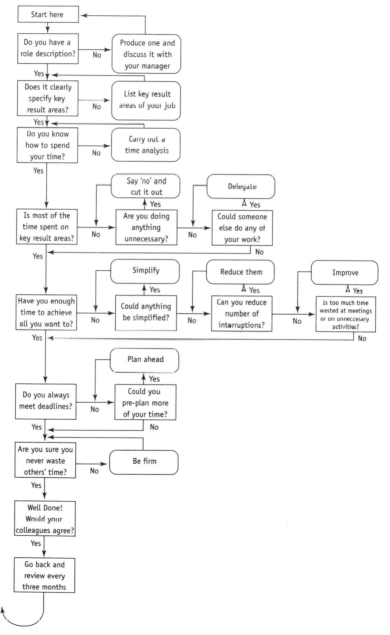

Managing people – a simple guide to assessing people

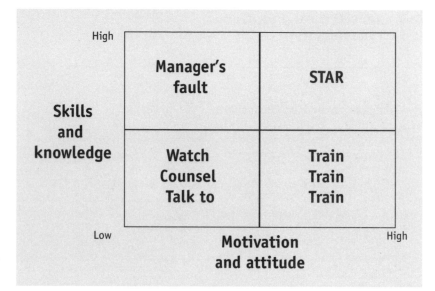

High performance team checklist

This checklist (opposite) is designed to help you think about the behaviour in your team. Read over the scales and place a cross on the scale that typifies the behaviour of your team.

1. Listening to others

Poor 0| 1| 2| 3| 4| 5| 6| 7| Excellent

2. Full participation by all team members

Poor 0| 1| 2| 3| 4| 5| 6| 7| Excellent

3. Decision making processes

Poor 0| 1| 2| 3| 4| 5| 6| 7| Excellent

4. Building and developing on team members ideas

Poor 0| 1| 2| 3| 4| 5| 6| 7| Excellent

5. Setting clear objectives and targets

Poor 0| 1| 2| 3| 4| 5| 6| 7| Excellent

6. Time management

Poor 0| 1| 2| 3| 4| 5| 6| 7| Excellent

7. Sensitivity of group members to the feelings of others

Poor 0| 1| 2| 3| 4| 5| 6| 7| Excellent

8. Handling conflicts within the team

Poor 0| 1| 2| 3| 4| 5| 6| 7| Excellent

9. Level of creativity and innovation

Poor 0| 1| 2| 3| 4| 5| 6| 7| Excellent

Consider the effectiveness of your team?

The key rules of assertiveness

- Know what you want.
- Prepare what you want to say.
- State what you want.
- Accept the risk element involved in being assertive.
- Stay calm and centred.
- Express your feelings with confidence.
- Give and accept praise without embarrassment.
- Give and accept fair and constructive criticism.
- Don't ramble – be succinct.
- Don't be devious or manipulative.
- Don't threaten or bully.
- Don't store up any negative feelings.
- Protect the integrity and dignity of others.

Listening skills checklist

Here are some practical measures to help you become a better listener:

- Listen carefully to the actual words being spoken.
- Occasionally ask for clarification, check your understanding of what is being said.
- Reflect any feelings and facts back to the speaker.
- Observe the speaker's body language.
- Don't let your emotions overtake you.
- Let the speaker finish, avoid interrupting the other person.
- Provide nods – show real interest.
- Maintain eye contact.

- Lean forward towards the speaker.
- Say "Uh, uh"..."yes"..."I see".
- Reserve judgment.
- Summarize the speaker from time to time.
- Don't switch off – stay alert.
- Don't drift onto another line of argument.
- Demonstrate respect, be courteous.
- Empathize with the speaker.
- Use sympathetic body language.

Other titles from Thorogood

Michael Williams

Mastering leadership

Michael Williams

Paperback ISBN: 1 85418 308 7/978-185418308-8
July 2006 • 220 pages • 2nd edition• £14.99

Fully updated and reformatted, this best-selling book reveals the key skills needed by any leader and shows how they can be used in practice, focusing on techniques for improving individual and organizational performance.

Written by an experienced practitioner with a proven track record of personal success, it enables mid to senior level managers to understand their own leadership style and provides guidance on how to develop a learning organization and how to be a successful mentor.

Contents include:

- Decision making

- A team effort

- Leader as mentor

- A master leader in action

- The changing world of management

- Historical balance sheet of debits and credits

- Mastering the organizational boundaries

- 'Mastery' – and beyond

THE AUTHOR

Michael Williams has run his own consultancy business since 1979 and specializes in leadership, management, team and organizational development for a wide range of organizations.

Mastering business planning and strategy

Paul Elkin

Paperback • 1 85418 072 X • 1998
280pp • £14.99
Hardback • 1 85418 190 4 • 1998
280pp • £19.99

A practical guide to developing successful business plans and strategies: provides techniques for profiling the business and its competition and analyzing the market and explores techniques for strategic thinking, option appraisal and decision-making.

Mastering marketing

Ian Ruskin-Brown

Paperback ISBN: 1 85418 323 0 /
978-185418323-1
July 2006 • 366 pages • 2nd edition • £14.99

A clearly written explanation of the core skills and concepts needed to market your products and services profitably. Updated and reformatted, this book offers more than short-term sales 'tricks', it provides techniques for building and maintaining a long-term profitable market position.

Particularly useful to managers newly appointed to the marketing department, or those wishing to liaise more closely with it, this book will also prove invaluable to owner-managers wishing to adopt a more structured approach to business development.

CONTENTS

1   The power of marketing
   - Effectiveness is more important than efficiency
   - The law of supply and demand

AUTHOR

Ian Ruskin-Brown is a highly experienced marketing consultant, with clients drawn from all over the world.

Gurus on people management

Sultan Kermally

Paperback 1 85418 320 6 • 2005 • 168pp • £14.99
Hardback 1 85418 325 7 • 2005 • 168pp • £24.99

A one-stop guide to the world's thought-leaders in people management. It summarizes the theory and contribution of each and assesses their pros and cons. But this is more than just a summary of key concepts: it offers valuable insights into their application and value with the help of real-life case studies which reflect some of the key management issues.

"A useful book for all managers."
BUSINESS EXECUTIVE

Leadership for leaders

Michael Williams

Paperback 1 85418 350 8 • 2005 • 192pp • £14.99
Hardback 1 85418 355 9 • 2005 • 192pp • £24.99

A ground-breaking book which challenges accepted 'norms' and establishes the seven key competencies required for successful leadership.

"A 'must read'."
BUSINESS EXECUTIVE (JOURNAL OF THE ASSOCIATION OF BUSINESS EXECUTIVES)

"Outstanding... clear, readable and full of sound advice."
JOHN ADAIR

"A very fine achievement."
YURY BOSHYK, CHAIRMAN, GLOBAL EXECUTIVE LEARNING

"... an informative and enjoyable read."
PAUL WINTER, CEO, THE LEADERSHIP TRUST

Focused on developing your potential

Falconbury, the sister company to Thorogood publishing, brings together the leading experts from all areas of management and strategic development to provide you with a comprehensive portfolio of action-centred training and learning.

We understand everything managers and leaders need to be, know and do to succeed in today's commercial environment. Each product addresses a different technical or personal development need that will encourage growth and increase your potential for success.

- Practical public training programmes
- Tailored in-company training
- Coaching
- Mentoring
- Topical business seminars
- Trainer bureau/bank
- Adair Leadership Foundation

The most valuable resource in any organization is its people; it is essential that you invest in the development of your management and leadership skills to ensure your team fulfil their potential. Investment into both personal and professional development has been proven to provide an outstanding ROI through increased productivity in both you and your team. Ultimately leading to a dramatic impact on the bottom line.

With this in mind Falconbury have developed a comprehensive portfolio of training programmes to enable managers of all levels to develop their skills in leadership, communications, finance, people management, change management and all areas vital to achieving success in today's commercial environment.

What Falconbury can offer you?

- Practical applied methodology with a proven results
- Extensive bank of experienced trainers
- Limited attendees to ensure one-to-one guidance
- Up to the minute thinking on management and leadership techniques
- Interactive training
- Balanced mix of theoretical and practical learning
- Learner-centred training
- Excellent cost/quality ratio

Falconbury In-Company Training

Falconbury are aware that a public programme may not be the solution to leadership and management issues arising in your firm. Involving only attendees from your organization and tailoring the programme to focus on the current challenges you face individually and as a business may be more appropriate. With this in mind we have brought together our most motivated and forward thinking trainers to deliver tailored in-company programmes developed specifically around the needs within your organization.

All our trainers have a practical commercial background and highly refined people skills. During the course of the programme they act as facilitator, trainer and mentor, adapting their style to ensure that each individual benefits equally from their knowledge to develop new skills.

Falconbury works with each organization to develop a programme of training that fits your needs.

Mentoring and coaching

Developing and achieving your personal objectives in the workplace is becoming increasingly difficult in today's constantly changing environment. Additionally, as a manager or leader, you are responsible for guiding colleagues towards the realization of their goals. Sometimes it is easy to lose focus on your short and long-term aims.

Falconbury's one-to-one coaching draws out individual potential by raising self-awareness and understanding, facilitating the learning and performance development that creates excellent managers and leaders. It builds renewed self-confidence and a strong sense of 'can-do' competence, contributing significant benefit to the organization. Enabling you to focus your energy on developing your potential and that of your colleagues.

Mentoring involves formulating winning strategies, setting goals, monitoring achievements and motivating the whole team whilst achieving a much improved work life balance.

Falconbury – Business Legal Seminars

Falconbury Business Legal Seminars specializes in the provision of high quality training for legal professionals from both in-house and private practice internationally.

The focus of these events is to provide comprehensive and practical training on current international legal thinking and practice in a clear and informative format.

Event subjects include, drafting commercial agreements, employment law, competition law, intellectual property, managing an in-house legal department and international acquisitions.

For more information on all our services please contact: Falconbury on +44 (0)20 7729 6677 or visit the website at: www.falconbury.co.uk.